DATE DUE

NOV 2 7 2018

WILD
ELEPHA
PRES
Washingt

D1468823

WILD
ELEPHANT
PRESS

PO Box 21351
Washington, DC 20009
www.wildelephantpress.com

Designed by Sandra Jonas

Printed in the United States of America
18 17 16 15 14 13   1 2 3 4 5 6

Publisher's Cataloguing-in-Publication Data

Crawford, J. Grigsby.
  The gringo : a memoir / J. Grigsby Crawford — Washington, DC : Wild Elephant Press, 2013.

  p. ; cm.

  ISBN: 9780988482272

  1. Peace Corps (U.S.) — Ecuador — Biography. 2. Ecotourism — Ecuador. 3. Crawford, J. Grigsby — Travel — Ecuador.

HC60.5 .C73 2013 918.66 — dc23

2012951864

Map of Ecuador by Pavalena/Shutterstock
Author photograph by Justin Schoolmaster

In memory of Barbara Crawford

COLOMBIA

PACIFIC
OCEAN

Olmedo

QUITO

ECUADOR

La Segua

Portoviejo

Guayaquil

Cuenca

PERU

Zumbi

Loja

N

0 Miles   125 Miles
0 Km   125 Km

For he said, "I have been a stranger
in a strange land."

—Exodus 2:22

TO THE READER

This is a work of nonfiction. I've reconstructed real conversations and events using memory and extensive note taking. The chronology of some minor events has been shifted to improve the flow. In some cases, I've changed people's names because my intention was to tell a story, not to embarrass anyone (although presenting an honest account means that a certain level of embarrassment for the characters involved—me included—is inevitable).

THE GRINGO

PART ONE

The Swamp

On the walls hung large posters showing light-skinned people and dark-skinned people smiling and working together in faraway corners of the world. The bottom of the photo read, "Life is calling. How far will you go?"

I sat waiting in the lobby of the Peace Corps Recruitment Office in Arlington, Virginia. After sending in my application a few weeks earlier, I'd been summoned for my face-to-face interview. It was January 2008.

Soon a nice young woman—the same one I'd met at a Peace Corps information seminar on my campus in December—came out to greet me and led me back to her office. We sat down and she launched into a monologue about her service in the Dominican Republic and how much she'd learned and how much she missed it and how she *really* needed to go overseas again.

She began asking me several questions, like how I felt about the need for personal space, how I felt about foreign languages and distant places, and if I had a girlfriend. I thought I was doing pretty well as she nodded intently and typed at her computer. I was wearing my best suit and tie.

Next she asked me for my first choice of region. In the Peace Corps application process, you don't get to choose anything—certainly not your country—but they at least ask you your regional preference.

I didn't hesitate. "Latin America," I said.

I'd fallen in love with that part of the world after studying abroad in Argentina during my junior year and traveling through much of the continent. I became obsessed with the language and culture and knew I'd try to get back there. Here was my opportunity.

My interviewer fretted a little over this. "That's our most competitive region," she told me. But then she nodded and said we'll see.

Somewhere along the way, while I was expounding on my passion for Latin America and my aptitude in Spanish, she stopped and yelped, "Oh shit!"

"What's wrong?" I said.

"Holy shit, oh my god," she said. She looked away from the computer screen and back to me. "Gosh, I'm sorry."

"What is it?"

"I was sending an email to someone," she said, "and instead of typing 'Obama,' I typed 'Osama' by mistake."

I let out a chuckle. "So, the previous ten minutes—were they actually part of the interview? I apologize, I just—"

"No, it's okay," she said. "Let's continue. I'm listening."

"Maybe if you email them back and explain the typo, they won't think—"

"No, it'll be fine."

The question-and-answer segment of the interview concluded with me admitting, despite my nice-looking transcript and Spanish knowledge and recommendations, that no, I did not in fact have any experience in any areas relevant to the Peace Corps. She kept typing but didn't respond.

I held my breath.

"Really?" she finally said. "No experience with agriculture or anything with nature?"

I stuttered out something about my mother having written environmental education curricula throughout her career, and the interviewer's response was, "But do *you* have any experience?"

Again, I said no. And I assumed that would be it and the ax would soon fall. She'd say the Foreign Service was calling my name, but the Peace Corps, on the other hand, didn't have any time for novices in the field of agriculture.

Instead she said, "Okay, I'm going to nominate you for a program in Latin America leaving this fall. Sometime between now and then you'll just need to get some experience relevant to environmental education."

I felt a wave of relief. "I'll be in Boulder, so that shouldn't be hard." My hometown in Colorado is famous for being a friend to all things nature.

She looked at me confused and said, "Okay, whatever."

Before I left, we went to a back room for what I considered my final leap of commitment to going forward with the Peace Corps: submitting my fingerprints as part of the standard background check.

As my interviewer took my ink-red fingers and rolled them one by one over the pages, she asked me what I was doing that weekend. We were standing so close to each other I couldn't turn my face toward hers because I'm pretty sure it would have been a nonprofessional distance. The tone of her question didn't make it any easier.

"Well," I said, staring straight ahead at the blank wall, "I won't be robbing any banks!"

"Huh?" she said.

"Oh, never mind. It's my brother's birthday. I think we'll be grabbing a nice dinner somewhere."

"Sounds cool."

We said our goodbyes and I walked back to the Rosslyn metro stop, snot freezing to my face in the cold, but with a slight hop in my step. I was in my final year of college. I was young. It was the twenty-first century. And I was about to get the chance to see what I was made of.

CHAPTER 2

When I graduated from college that spring, I assumed I'd be departing in a few months, as the Peace Corps had told me. I thought everything was all set.

But one thing the Peace Corps does to weed out applicants is complicate the process. They don't make the interview or application particularly tough or selective per se—they just make it a pain in the ass.

I'd been writing for a political magazine my senior year and right before graduation I told my editor that I'd be leaving for the Peace Corps. He said, with a chuckle, that the neighborhood where he grew up in Brooklyn could use some Peace Corps volunteers, then wished me luck. By telling him this instead of asking for a job, I'd put all my eggs in the Peace Corps basket. That made my extended application process particularly stressful.

I had made the mistake of admitting on the hundred-question-long yes-or-no portion of the medical application that, yes, I had been to therapy in the previous five years. It had actually been about four and a half years since I'd seen anyone, so I didn't think it was a big deal. I recall thinking that with the prospect of deep isolation and culture shock, they should be more concerned about the people who have *never* seen a psychologist.

Still, checking off yes in the therapy-within-the-last-five-years box set off a bureaucratic shitstorm that took several months to resolve.

It included ringing up the Boulder therapist I'd seen back in high school so she could fill out fifteen or so pages on the ins and outs of my psyche. (She was shocked and confused to later find out that they had summoned all this information without having me sign a release; she just assumed I had because it would have been nuts and arguably illegal to give them the information otherwise.) It had been so long since I'd seen her that she had to access her storage facility to pull out my records. I eventually got over the frustration of having to do all this, realizing that at least they weren't letting in the crazies. I faxed over the forms.

But that wasn't enough. They told me I would have to fill out even more psychological paperwork, including a personal statement guaranteeing the Peace Corps that I had no intention of killing myself—not then or anytime in the future.

It wasn't the most dignified personal essay I'd ever written.

Then there were more headaches involving doctor's notes, illegible faxes, and further paperwork, all to reassure them that I wasn't unstable, wasn't taking medicine, and was *really* sure that I didn't feel like killing myself. Meanwhile, they checked and rechecked my college transcript to make sure I had really taken all the Spanish classes I said I had. (With Latin America being so competitive, they told me, they couldn't waste their time with people who didn't already have a solid Spanish background.)

At one point, I was informed that two of the check boxes on my physical evaluation were left blank. The first, "breasts," was omitted by my doctor because he wrongfully assumed that it only concerned females. The second—"anus"—was in need of revision because instead of a check mark over the "no" problem box, my doctor had written "OK."

I went back to the doctor, where he determined my breasts were in satisfactory condition. Next, we addressed the second outstanding check box on the form, completing one of the quickest and most awkward doctor visits of my life. With the stroke of my doctor's pen, my asshole was clear and I was ready for the Peace Corps.

A FULL SEVEN MONTHS AFTER I applied and interviewed, they told me I'd no longer be leaving in September, as originally promised. I was pushed back a few months to January of the following year—a full year after I'd applied—but as a consolation, I'd find out in just a couple of weeks which country I'd be serving in. In late September, I was finally invited to a Peace Corps post: Bolivia.

Though it was landlocked and looked eerily like Afghanistan in parts due to miles of rugged highland countryside, I was excited about Bolivia. It was second only to Haiti for most impoverished nation in the Western Hemisphere, but I'd been there the summer before and found it charming. I'd even been to the place where our training was to be held—a city called Cochabamba, located roughly in the middle of the country. A friend of mine from college lived there with his family, and I remember getting off the eight-hour bus ride from La Paz and thinking, *Now* this *is South America.*

The excitement was short-lived. A few weeks after I received my invitation (and sent off an updated résumé and mission statement to my future program managers in Cochabamba), news developed regarding civil unrest in Bolivia. The U.S. ambassador was kicked out of the country by the Bolivian government and the Peace Corps soon followed.

I later found out one of the main reasons the Peace Corps had to be pulled out of there, despite the fact that the majority of the country was insulated from the civil unrest: During an information session with someone from the U.S. Embassy, a foreign service officer casually mentioned that if any volunteers came across Cuban or Venezuelan nationals in or around their sites, they should report it. The Peace Corps country director quickly interrupted and said that the officer's directive was completely wrong and also illegal. But apparently a few volunteers rushed to the nearest Internet café and put it on their blogs, only to have their comments catch the eye of some Bolivians and eventually their socialist president, Evo Morales, leading him to go around the country likening Peace Corps volunteers to "little spies." I'm still impressed that volunteers' blogs were actually being read.

At this news, I fell into another funk. Once again, I didn't know where—or when—I was heading abroad. I was so frustrated with the Peace Corps that I would have found something else to do—if that something existed. About this time, the U.S. economy was collapsing, which was awful news for everyone except Barack Obama's presidential campaign.

A month later I finally learned via email that they would be sending me to Ecuador in February. A quick Google search gave me some facts about the country, including its currency (the U.S. dollar) and size (nearly the same, in land mass, as Colorado). I suppose it was a small bonus that Ecuador was slightly less likely to implode politically and socially than, say, Bolivia. I was especially excited because I hadn't gone there when I traveled the continent two years prior, so here was my chance to fill in a blank on the map. *At least I'm going somewhere*, I thought. By then I would have said yes to any country or any region if it meant finally getting off my ass and leaving.

I sent out notes to my family and some friends telling them about my impending adventure. Everyone said good luck. To most in my family, I suppose it fit in with their idea of me always doing something off the beaten path. My mom, though, kept repeating how she couldn't believe I was voluntarily subjecting myself to two things I'd never done well with: loneliness and boredom. No one else offered much commentary, but my mother's words would later echo loudly.

Others wanted to know *why*. After asking where Ecuador was on the map and what language was spoken there, they wanted to know why I would sign up for over two years of my life. As I'd come to find out from other volunteers, you had the reasons you told others—wanting to help people, see the world, experience a completely different culture. And then there were the real reasons, which you kept to yourself, partially because they didn't sound as good in conversation and partially because you (at least I did) spent lots of time thinking about it even after you got there, before narrowing it down to something you thought made sense when said aloud.

I went for all those reasons I told people, too, but I really went to test myself. I knew it would be dirty and rough and lonely—and I wanted to see how I'd react. I figured that I'd learn something about myself—some romantic truth I wouldn't be able to get by sitting at a desk somewhere. This last part was perhaps a bit naïve, but probably no more so than the entire premise of young Americans moving to poorer countries to show the people there how it's done.

I would be shipping out on February 25, three days after my twenty-third birthday.

CHAPTER 3

First they brought us to Washington, D.C., for "staging," beginning a seventy-two-hour whirlwind that ended in a tiny town high in the Andes. Spending my final hours in the country in D.C. made it a bittersweet hello-goodbye to the city where I'd gone to college and lived four of the last five years.

I arrived on a Monday, and the next day, forty-five of us were herded into the banquet room of the Holiday Inn in Georgetown. I saw people in teary-eyed cell phone conversations with parents. I saw young women lugging giant rolling bags you'd expect to see at the loading dock for a spring break cruise. I saw cargo pants and vests and shiny new hiking boots. I saw brand-spanking-new water bottles that looked sturdy enough to survive a nuclear blast. I saw happy faces, excited faces, scared faces, friendly faces. I saw name tags stuck on breast pockets of REI shirts.

We were all introduced via several icebreaker activities and a crash course in what it meant to be in the Peace Corps. I found out that we weren't yet "volunteers," because you had to make it through training and "swear in" to earn that label. After we landed in Ecuador and up until the point of swearing in, we'd be known as "trainees."

In an awkward turn of events, the emcee—a returned volunteer from Morocco (her service was "incredible")—took a few moments at the end of her final session to say something along the lines of, "Now, if you're having any doubts, if you think this might not be for you, well, then here's your chance to say, okay, you know what, I think I'll pass and head back home." She paused, standing at the front of the room and waiting in silence as if she actually expected someone to get up from one of the eight circular tables and say, "I'm outta here."

All of us soon-to-be-trainees kind of glanced around the room at one another to see if someone would actually get up and skulk out. The silence probably lasted thirty seconds, but it felt like several minutes. The head of staging then clapped her hands together in front of her the way cheerleaders do and said, "All right! You guys are going to have the time of your lives."

I kept scanning the room for anyone who indeed wanted to go home but who found standing up alone in that room more terrifying than whatever lay ahead of us in Ecuador. It was tough to tell. (In fact, scanning the room for the terrified and confused was something I'd do nearly every day during our two months of training to amuse or inform myself, or both.) I didn't find out until afterward that earlier in the day someone in our training group had indeed arrived at the hotel in D.C. only to turn around and go home hours later.

The rest of the day consisted of even more icebreakers and skits designed to teach us about several Peace Corps policies. Writing a blog? We had to notify administration so it could get reviewed for content. Taking a vacation? Not in our first or last three months of service. Feeling sick? We'd be given medical kits upon our arrival in Quito, the capital city. And so on.

For one of our activities, we were handed a notebook full of questions to ask one another. Some called for facts, such as what year the Peace Corps was founded (1961!). Others were more open ended, such as, "What did you do in preparation for your service?" Most people took this question more literally and said things like, "I sold my car," or "I said all the proper goodbyes." But one guy, walking around the room in hiking boots and a fleece vest, told us, without irony, that he'd "found inner peace." For the next two years, everyone called him Inner Peace Mark.

Later in the day, I found out that the Peace Corps had the wrong address for my home of record and had been sending critical information to a random address in Northwest D.C. for the previous ten months. One of the former volunteers helping with our staging said she'd take care of it, no problem. It would take them over a year to correct this.

We woke up early Wednesday morning and they shuttled us to the airport. Our flight landed late that night at the Quito airport where the Peace Corps country director and other office personnel met us. From then on, we were known as Omnibus 101. I still don't know the reason for the term "omnibus," but all it meant was that we were the 101st group of trainees to arrive in Peace Corps Ecuador.

CHAPTER 4

For the next nine weeks, I lived in Olmedo, a tiny village tucked in a lush valley underneath the snow-capped Cayambe Volcano, which towers to nearly 19,000 feet. We were all sprinkled about in groups of four or five across various communities that surrounded Cayambe, the city where our training sessions took place.

One of the first things we did was take language exams. After getting grilled over the phone for months on end about my transcript and language classes, I was really sweating it, thinking that my four semesters of college Spanish would be the worst in our group and that I'd be laughed out of training. On the first day, it became clear that at least a dozen trainees had no Spanish background at all.

Training was a mixture of chaos and bureaucratic battles among program managers, program officers, program specialists, training specialists, training managers, logistics coordinators, and volunteer trainers. I'm still not sure what any of their specific roles were. They all desperately wanted to seem in charge and be taken seriously. Some tried extra hard to let the trainees and volunteers know that they "got it."

And it should have come as no surprise that somewhere in there was an acronym bonanza of epic proportions. It was only a matter of time before things like COS, CD, PTO, PCMO, ET, PCPP, EFT, PCV, PCT, AO, PM, EAP, and CBT actually meant something to us.

(And you must make the decision very quickly whether you want to be the type of volunteer who gives a shit and uses these terms on a regular basis.)

A gaggle of maybe a half-dozen language trainers were each assigned to one of our training communities. Their job was to not only guide our daily Spanish lessons, but also help integrate us into Ecuadorian culture. Some of these guys turned out to be jokesters and I became friendly with a few of them. One trainer enjoyed teaching us dirty jokes and swear words and giving us insights into the complicated nature of Ecuadorian women. On the latter subject, he pointed out that no women—and certainly no men—enjoyed using condoms. It was, he said, like eating a candy without taking off the wrapper. A few months down the road, after training ended, he told me with a shrug that he was a new father.

During the initial days, the head training manager informed us that during our free time (which was either weekends or the few hours after training sessions ended each day), we were not allowed to congregate in groups of more than six. In addition to that rule, she explained that we'd have to be on the bus back to our homestays *immediately* after training sessions ended, which equated to a curfew of about 6:15 p.m. If we thought we could meet up with other volunteers at the bars or, god forbid, do so in groups of greater than six, we were sorely mistaken.

ALSO NEAR THE BEGINNING OF training, we got our inaugural visit from Nurse Nancy, head of the Peace Corps Ecuador medical office. Nurse Nancy was a rail-thin blonde who chain-smoked and ate lunch every day at the Quito McDonald's. She had a high-pitched voice and looked at us with wide-eyed, faux enthusiasm. From our vantage point, enthusiasm was hard to come by when the topic was a (stomach-turning) STD slideshow or a speech on the possibilities of stomach viruses and intestinal worms.

About a month later, she showed us a video interview with a

woman who'd been raped the night of her swearing in as a volunteer in Quito. Following that was an '80s-era documentary featuring a half-dozen volunteers who'd contracted HIV/AIDS during their services. It was unsettling. Each session ended with Nurse Nancy clapping her hands, shining a spooky smile, and saying, "Are we excited or what!"

Early on, she conducted one-on-one interviews to get to know each of us personally. When my turn came, I went over and sat next to her on a bench outside the Quonset hut–looking building where our training sessions took place.

"So, how we doin'?" she said.

"I'm fine, thank you," I said. For some reason, every time I met new Peace Corps personnel, I felt compelled to come across as well as possible, as if I were still in the interview process.

Nurse Nancy then asked me a battery of questions, such as how I was feeling, how I dealt with stress, and if I was "gay, straight, or *other*, hehehehe."

We arrived at what I assume was the auxiliary portion of the get-to-know-each-other interview, and Nurse Nancy scrolled her finger down the page as if she were looking over the highlights of an intelligence briefing for the real meat of the information.

"Well, well, well, I see here it says you've had some counseling in the past," she said. Even though it was clearly information I had provided them, I couldn't help but sense a bit of a *gotcha* tone.

"Yes," I said. "Nearly five years ago."

"Is there anything you'd like to talk about with me?" she asked.

"No, that's okay."

That wasn't all. Nurse Nancy's finger scrolled some more. Then it flipped over to the second page, and then flipped again back to the first too quickly for me to see what was there.

"It also says here you've had some dealings with depression," she began. I raised my eyebrows in anticipation of the next words that could possibly come out of her mouth. "You know," she said, "we have options for counseling and that sort of thing, so you can always tell us what's going on."

"That sounds nice," I said. And she nearly interrupted me with what was on the tip of her tongue.

"Because, you know," said Nurse Nancy, "we don't want you out there in your site in the middle of nowhere getting all depressed and then thinking to yourself, 'Hey—there's a tree branch, I think I'll go hang myself on it!'" She let out something between a giggle and a hiccup and managed to smile.

I just looked at her.

"You know," she said.

Possibly sensing the awkwardness in the air—but probably not—Nurse Nancy said a few moments later, "And, well, since you've had some, uh, *problems*, in this whole area, we're putting you on doxycycline for malaria prophylaxis, instead of Lariam. Lariam sometimes makes people have psychotic episodes."

Actual doctors back home had told me as much, so I nodded in agreement. She added that since I'd "dealt" with some of the "problems" she mentioned, my Peace Corps file would be labeled such-and-such. (Here she quickly rattled off a combination of letters and numbers that undoubtedly corresponded to some government code for people who'd once succumbed to teenage angst and consequently been prescribed one or several antidepressants.)

"What's that classification mean?" I asked.

"It's just, you know, the way we'll mark you—I mean your file."

"Do other people see this?" After my application ordeal, I'd become somewhat of an expert on the medical privacy laws of the United States, so this piqued my interest.

"No need to worry," she said. "It's just a classification on your file."

"I understand that, but should I be concerned about who can see that and find out my medical information?"

"Oh, no, sweetie. And—whoops," she said, looking at her watch in a grand gesture, "time's up!"

Somewhere during that conversation, I surmised that keeping the medical office completely informed about my health might be a high-risk activity.

CHAPTER 5

B efore leaving for Ecuador, a friend back home introduced me to
an older man who'd been a Peace Corps volunteer in Central
America in the '80s. In addition to serving there, he'd later lived in
Ecuador for several years. One night in Boulder, we sat down over
beers and he told me about his experience, including the horrors of
what training was like in those days. He described a hard-core boot
camp–like affair the Peace Corps used to weed out the weak. It even
took place on a military base where they could see soldiers doing their
own training on an adjacent field. (In those earlier days, training was
held inside the United States, and upon swearing in, the volunteers
flew to their country of service and went directly to their sites.)

In preparation for building latrines or digging wells in Central
America, Peace Corps trainees had to rappel down three-story buildings, take aerobic endurance tests, and do simulated drowning exer-
cises. It was almost as if the Peace Corps' intent, he said, was to get as
many people to quit as possible. It was literally survival of the fittest.

When they weren't being timed in the mile run or learning jujitsu
or whatever else was included, trainees were constantly monitored
by a team of psychologists. Holding a clipboard, they would come up
to a trainee, stare at him or her for several seconds, jot down a few
notes, then walk away.

Some trainees cracked. Perhaps they couldn't take the physical endurance or maybe it was the psychological scrutiny, but in the middle of an exercise, they would announce that they'd had enough and it was the last that anyone would see of them. Most, however, passed. They made it through training, swore in, and departed for their country of service, where they practiced a grand total of zero of the martial expertise they'd acquired in the several weeks prior.

With that in mind, I went into training prepared to kick ass. In a matter of minutes, however, I discovered that training in the *twenty-first century* Peace Corps had about as much in common with boot camp as did a chapter meeting for the local Cub Scouts. The gradual pussification of the Peace Corps in recent decades had caused a 180-degree turn that took training from a genuinely rugged ordeal to something like college orientation, only lamer.

So, here we are in the giant concrete building for our training sessions, where we sit on campfire-style benches and start the day off with a group sing-along.

Here we are treated to a puppet show explaining what we should do in the event of a volcanic eruption (a serious possibility in Ecuador, which has had notable eruptions as recently as the late '90s). Trainees laugh and clap and take pictures while the trainees-cum-puppeteers show off their best Elmo voices. Raucous laughter continues as a gang of talking sock hands describe how quickly we might suffocate on ash or lose our legs to highly viscous molten rock. It's a real gas.

Here's a series of interpretive skits to illustrate what we should do preceding an evacuation scenario (the exact type of event, in other words, that had led to my being there instead of in Bolivia). Inner Peace Mark demands that we sing our script to the melody of Billy Joel's "The Longest Time." (We absolutely nail it.)

Here we are in small groups breaking into song and dance again to present reports of the mini projects we've done in our training communities. (The winning group got to perform in front of the ambassador.)

Here we are treated to an impromptu crazy dance party, before 9 a.m., and our language facilitators dress up like clowns and spray us with confetti and glitter. (I later find out this is somewhat of an Ecuadorian tradition, but still.)

Here we are standing in a large circle for a diversity session and taking turns explaining what makes us *different*. One trainee says, inexplicably, "I am Hispanic, though I have the good fortune not to look it." Luckily, the Ecuadorian language facilitators don't hear it, but the few Hispanic Americans in our training group do (and will remain perplexed and offended by the comment, even over a year later).

Here we are beginning the day with a game of Simon Says and the loser has to get up in front of the group and sing.

Here we are playing a version of hot potato for an information session on human trafficking.

Here we are making not an actual composting toilet, but a scale model of one, using nearby sticks and twigs.

Here we are baking cake with our language facilitator.

Here I am asked to dress in feathery chaps and a cowboy hat to help with an indigenous dance routine for a session on Ecuadorian culture.

And eventually: Here we are having our names pulled out of a hat and announced like we're contestants on *The Price Is Right*. Here we are running over rose petals and through a tunnel formed by human arms. Here we are getting handed an envelope with our names written decoratively on the outside and our site assignments written on the inside. Here we are bursting through the tunnel toward a sign that says, "How Far Will You Go?" Answer: ten feet away toward a giant map of Ecuador taped to the floor where we stand on our corresponding part of the country. Here we are catching our breath and brushing off the rose petals as we find out where we'll spend the next two years of our lives.

I would be heading for the coast, which in Ecuador referred not just to the beaches, but to the entire western third of the country—a humid flatland squeezed between the Andes and the Pacific Ocean.

CHAPTER 6

A couple of weeks after arriving in Ecuador, we traveled to a farm an hour outside Cayambe for what the Peace Corps called a "technical training." We spent the day in groups of six going from station to station doing things like making a seedbed, raking clean a field so a greenhouse could be built, and turning guinea pig urine into a good fertilizer. Guinea pigs are also considered a delicacy in this area of the Andes, and at lunch we all watched one get prepared for eating, which included a grisly skull crushing.

In the afternoon, we continued working until we got to our last station of the day: tree grafting. Our co-trainer—one of the four volunteers who spent the final months of his service helping prepare the fresh recruits—had a fat dip of chewing tobacco in his lip as he proceeded to explain the several different methods of grafting.

"How many trees did you graft over the last two years?" I asked.

He looked up at me and then turned to discharge a mouthful of golden-brown saliva.

"I learned how to graft trees this morning," he said, "on Wikipedia."

THROUGHOUT THOSE WEEKS, WE'D GET visits from current volunteers, already neck-deep in their service or approaching the end. Some of them came to describe their projects to us. Then during breaks between sessions, over cookies and soda, they'd lean in to whisper things like, "Forget all this shit, man. When you get out to your site, everything changes. They [Peace Corps personnel in Quito] will forget about you and it's a complete shit show," or "Dude, don't take your malaria medicine, that's a load of shit," or "Dude, fuck that policy about sending a text message every single time you leave your site. I traveled this entire country without telling those assholes where I was."

During safety and security sessions, current volunteers would tell us their cautionary tales of getting robbed on buses or mugged in the major city Guayaquil or having their backpack stolen in an elaborate spilled-mustard scheme. One story that stuck out in my mind came from a woman roughly my age who'd been located near Guayaquil for the previous year. She stood up in front of our group of over forty, seated in a semicircle on those campground-style benches, and talked about how she and two visiting friends got into a cab late one night. The next thing they knew, she said, the cab slowed to a stop, and men with guns got out of a car in front of them and forced their way into the cab. With the gun barrels pressed against their temples, the women were driven to the nearest ATM. After draining the money from all their bank accounts, the gunmen dropped them out of the cab in an unfamiliar neighborhood far on the outskirts of Guayaquil. Without money or cell phones, the three of them were left to knock on a stranger's door and beg for help.

By the time she finished telling her story, she was shaking slightly, clearly traumatized at having to relive the details of her "express kidnapping" for our edification. Normally, when these storytelling sessions—usually concerning run-of-the-mill larcenies—ended, we trainees politely clapped as the speaker stepped down off the stage. This time, clapping seemed out of place, so instead we slow clapped, like you see in cliché sports movies. The clapping faded and the woman walked outside. She didn't stick around for a meet-and-greet session during free time.

The safety and security sessions were usually capped off with some crime and rape statistics and a chitchat from the country director about how we'd be totally fucked if we got caught doing drugs or messing with an underage girl. If we thought we'd be cut some slack or some diplomatic strings would be pulled for us in the event of getting caught up in anything even slightly resembling a Led Zeppelin backstage party, we were wrong.

Other official policies (easily referenced in the Peace Corps Ecuador *Volunteer Handbook*) were served to us in heaping doses. Chief among them was the Out of Site Policy. If we thought volunteer travel in country was going to be a free-for-all like it was under the previous country director, we had to think again. We would not be allowed to leave our sites for the first three months. This news was received by the trainees with so much devastation you'd have thought it was a personal insult.

After the three months, however, we would be allotted six out-of-site days a month, which could be used in no more than three-day/two-night consecutive chunks. If we planned to leave our site, we had to send a text message to our program manager, our assistant program manager, and our community counterpart, both when we left and when we returned.

This permissible time away was most certainly not for just shits and giggles. As stated in our policy handbook, we needed to use those days primarily for activities like buying groceries, going to the bank, and getting supplies. The list of acceptable excuses for leaving included "mental health days" and ended with "etc."

As with all other rule breaking, the penalty for not adhering to any of the aforementioned out-of-site bylaws was "Administrative Separation"—a fancy term for getting kicked out. (Administrative Separation entailed getting immediately pulled from your site and sent on a flight back home after spending about thirty-six hours in Quito filling out paperwork concerning your incomplete service.) The way the country director and training manager kept repeating the term "Administrative Separation" and writing it on training materials gave it a chilling, Orwellian connotation. It was as though Administrative Separation was a living thing—a burly monster lurking over your shoulder, ready to catch you in the act of breaking a rule so it could black-flag you from ever getting a government job and, among other things, ruin your life.

If we operated any motorized vehicle, we would be Administratively Separated.

If we failed to take our malaria medications, we would be Administratively Separated.

If we entered any of the areas along the Colombian border that were off-limits to personnel in the American Mission, we would be Administratively Separated.

If we engaged in any public nudity, we would be Administratively Separated. (Although, the *Volunteer Handbook* omitted the word "public" before "nudity," making for an amusing predicament.)

If we so much as whiffed any illegal drugs, we would be Administratively Separated and left to the Ecuadorian authorities to be dealt with in ways that I'm sure would have made *Midnight Express* look like a picnic. The country director added with a wry smile that if we got in trouble for drugs, the U.S. government would *not* help us get out of jail.

In fact, if there were even *rumors* in the communities about illegal drug use by a volunteer, he or she would be Administratively Separated.

If we engaged in sexual contact with someone under the age of eighteen, we would be Administratively Separated. We were also told—incorrectly, I later learned—that this would be a violation of the United States Protect Act.

If we went to certain beaches, we would be Administratively Separated.

If we hung out in the Mariscal, the grotesquely backpacker-friendly party neighborhood of Quito, past 2 a.m., we would be—*wait for it!*—Administratively Separated.

If we went to Baños, a town at the base of an active volcano that oddly attracts lots of tourists, we would be Administratively

Separated. (A woman in our group found this out the hard way after three months in site.)

Medical Separations were kind of like benign cousins of Administrative Separations; they were mostly for people who got serious injuries and couldn't recover in a reasonable enough time to return to their country of service. Regarding Medical Separations, there was a lot of ambiguous language in the handbook, but I was amused by one topic: If volunteers got one abortion, they were okay. If they got a second, they would likely be . . . Medically Separated.

Last but not least, if we acted in any way that compromised the integrity of the Peace Corps, we would be Administratively Separated—a vague rule, but it struck me as the best one in the handbook because it could have replaced all the others, thereby treating us like the adults they had trusted enough to accept into the Peace Corps.

We would come to find out later that, even when in violation of said policies, volunteers were never truly *kicked out*. Instead, they were given a forty-eight-hour grace period in which they could choose to Early Terminate, thus avoiding a blackballing from all government jobs forever.

CHAPTER 7

From the training facility in Cayambe, I had a forty-five-minute bus ride back to my host family's home in Olmedo. The village has an elevation of around 10,000 feet, making it chilly at night with a scorching sun during the day, much like the Colorado mountain towns where I skied growing up. Four other trainees were scattered about Olmedo, living with other host families. The five of us had the same language trainer, Javier, who also lived there.

The small town had one big cobblestone street down the middle with a few dirt side streets. The quiet emptiness of Olmedo was occasionally interrupted by pickup trucks rumbling down the street with screeching bullhorns on top. The words coming from the bullhorn were too fast and shrill for me to make out. I once asked Javier what they were saying. "They're giving some sort of political message," he said. He paused for a moment. "Oh, no, wait, they're selling pumpkins."

On the first day that I arrived at my host family's house, Papi Juan, the patriarch, greeted me wearing a University of Colorado ball cap. I came to find out that Papi Juan was one of the most popular men in town. He was kind, smiled a lot, and had a big chuckle that would make his dentures nearly fall from his mouth. Papi Juan was fun—and an alcoholic.

He said that I was the fourth *gringuito* they had hosted and apparently not the first from Colorado. As it turned out, the previous

Peace Corps trainee was, like me, from Boulder. I later discovered he also went to my high school.

Parked in front of the house was a former school bus that Papi Juan owned and used every day to take laborers back and forth between the flower-picking factories. These were basically industrial-size greenhouses where Papi Juan described the workers being badly treated and breathing in chemicals all day while they picked and sorted flowers that got shipped off to North America.

The host family took a liking to me right away. After one try at pronouncing the name I go by, they asked me what my other name was. My first name, James, which only gets used by credit card companies and substitute teachers, proved to be much easier for them to pronounce, so that's what they called me.

I lived in the same room of their house that the previous gringos had slept in; each night I fell asleep below a wall shrine of photos and souvenirs dedicated to the Peace Corps trainees that had come before me. It was a four-room house, including my bedroom, Papi Juan and his wife's bedroom, the kitchen, and a living area decorated with a serious amount of Catholic paraphernalia.

In preparation for my arrival, I could tell they'd tidied things up, including waxing the floors with leaded diesel. A combination of that aroma and the high altitude usually meant that before going to bed, I'd tucker out after about ten push-ups on my bedroom floor.

My second weekend there, Papi Juan took me fishing a few hours away. We drove through the gorgeous *paramo* scenery of shrubs and clear mountain lakes, and when we passed through the clouds on an extra steep section of road, the car almost broke down. Sucking down a cigarette, Papi Juan instructed me to get out and run alongside the car so it could make it over the mountain pass.

Another weekend, I came back late from drinking with fellow trainees in a Cayambe bar, only to find Papi Juan about ten times drunker than I was. He roped me into listening to a slurring soliloquy delivered as a half-smoked cigarette dangled from his lips and he demanded more beer from his wife. Before long, things devolved into a slobbering slush of words and tears when Papi Juan remarked that I'd be leaving him in only a few short weeks to go live with those "monkeys" on the coast. (Ecuadorians of the highlands or Amazon regions refer to those living on the coast as monkeys—*monos*—either because of thinly veiled racism or because of the coast-dwellers' huge consumption of bananas; the first time I heard them talking about *monos*, it took several minutes before I realized they were talking about humans.)

Papi Juan put his head down on the dining room table like a man in the throes of grief. When he looked up, I saw tears streaking down his face. His cigarette stained the wood. "You're like my son," he said. "And now you're leaving me. LEAVING ME!" He banged the table with his fist. He cried more and hugged me and asked me if I wanted a cigarette. I told him I didn't smoke. He told me his family was going to miss me a lot and that he loved tobacco and beer very much. I would miss them, too, I said. His crying let up and I told him that it was going to be okay and that I would visit them every chance I got.

Papi Juan kept on crying. Throughout this time, his dentures (I hadn't confirmed they were false teeth until he'd had a fish bone–choking episode a few days before and launched them onto the kitchen table) kept slipping out of his mouth. He cried and mumbled some more and lit up another cigarette. All the while, I, his wife, his daughter, and his two tiny grandchildren looked on and said nothing.

One Saturday morning, Papi Juan sat at breakfast talking about the training communities where the other Peace Corps trainees lived.

"I don't know how they can live there," he said. He was referring to other villages tucked in the same valley, below the Cayambe Volcano. He went on, "The people in those communities—it's another class of people"—he paused for effect—"they're *indigenous people*." I left the house to go play basketball and returned that afternoon to see Papi Juan bathing nude by the washbasin in the backyard.

Most of the time, things were fine in that house. They treated me—their little gringo—with a reverence that was usually flattering.

(Though sometimes it was insulting, like when they thought I was incapable of boiling water on my own.) I became friends with Papi Juan's wife, Marta, who would sit me down and treat me to some monologues of her own. In one, she shared with me a complete breakdown of their finances. In another, I learned that Marta's sister had saved up money and moved to Spain, but no one had heard from her since. Earlier that week in training, we'd attended a presentation on the different forms of human trafficking in Ecuador, including hoaxes that led women to believe they were getting a deal with a visa and flight to Spain. They were sold into sex slavery instead and held captive for the rest of their lives.

AT THIS POINT IN TRAINING, it was time for each trainee to take a three-day visit to his or her site to find out what life would be like for the next two years. Mine was named La Segua, located just outside the city of Chone in the coastal province of Manabí.

On the day I received my site assignment, my program manager—that is, the head of the Department of Natural Resource Conservation in Peace Corps Ecuador—pulled me aside. His last name was Winkler. He was a squirrelly man with the physique of a horse jockey who was the product of an Ecuadorian mother of German descent and an American Peace Corps volunteer father.

As with all sites, Winkler explained, a community-based group in La Segua had filed an application with the Peace Corps Ecuador office requesting the services of a volunteer. Volunteers were allowed to read these applications, which contained some details about the community and the family they'd be living with.

Unlike most of my fellow trainees, though, I wouldn't be replacing an outgoing volunteer. Typically, a newcomer went to a site that a current volunteer was about to leave, creating an endless cycle of gringos for that village. But in my case, I'd be the first gringo ever in La Segua, Manabí.

Winkler had some additional thoughts on La Segua. "Your site is the most rugged one we have here in Peace Corps Ecuador," he told me. "We think you can take it."

I felt proud that somehow in the previous six weeks of being bored and annoyed, I'd given them the impression that I could cut it in their most "rugged" site.

"What do you mean by 'rugged'?" I asked him.

"Well, Chone—it's kind of like the Wild West of Ecuador," he said. "It's just rough and the people are known for being a little aggressive—you'll see."

"That sounds good," I said. It was just what I had gone there for.

It had been a long journey already. As a friend of mine stated, after all those months of waiting and putting up with the bullshit of the application process, it would have taken "something really fucked" to make him bail before his two years were up. I agreed. I was ready to set off into the rugged beyond.

CHAPTER 8

Firation it's the heat. The heat is what hits you first.

La Segua sits about an hour inland from the coastline and belongs to a large wasteland of sweaty, beaten terrain that gets pounded, in intervals, by heat and rain. Winkler had remarked that it was the Wild West of Ecuador. To me it felt like swamplands in the Deep South—the *antebellum* South.

The province of Manabí is the anti–bread basket of Ecuador. It's low, if not the lowest, in all the statistics you want to be high in—literacy, production, health—and high in all the ones you want to be low in—poverty, domestic violence, hunger. The people there wake up every morning and get kicked in the face by life. Every day is a battle and they're losing.

As a Peace Corps site, it was perfect. You name it—plumbing, running water, stable electricity, post–elementary school educations—and they didn't have it. The bar was so low that the possibilities for improving the quality of life seemed endless.

Approaching La Segua from the north, you pass a giant landfill between the highway and the ocean. The toxic runoff from the fill drains down toward a shrimp farm leading out to sea. Wisps of smoke and sick-looking pelicans perch atop the mounds of smoldering gray waste in a postapocalyptic image.

The chief export of Manabí, technically speaking, is bananas.

But if you ask anyone else in Ecuador, the chief export of Manabí is laziness. It's the unique brand of stereotype that, if true, is at least forgivable. On either side of the highway, I saw an endless landscape of potbellied men swinging from hammocks, with a machete in one hand and a beer in the other. In the heat and with so little going on, their sloth is understandable—not to mention that with every meal being a variation on rice and plantain, there was literally a finite amount of energy your body could exert.

It is a strange place with strange stories. But mostly, it is a land of distrust.

BEFORE WE LEFT CAYAMBE FOR our short visits, our program managers gave us a batch of information about our sites and the people we'd be teamed up with, known as our counterparts.

These locals were described as heads of organizations or the community. Among other things, they were in charge of finding us our initial housing for the first few months. In addition to working with us, they were, in a sense, responsible for our well-being. For instance, if we ever left our site—even for a day—we were supposed to notify them when we left and when we returned.

Throughout training, counterparts had been described to us as figures of authority, so you can imagine my surprise when my "boss" turned out to be a child.

I stood on the dirty sidewalk of the bus station and called my counterpart to tell him I'd arrived.

"Where are you?" he said.

I told him I was standing over in the corner of the parking lot.

There was a pause. "Oh, I see you," he said. "I'm walking toward you now."

"I don't see you yet. Are you sure you see me?"

When I said this, he was standing about five yards away—directly in front of me. Expecting to see an adult, I'd been looking right past him.

He was twenty years old (and fresh off a university degree in tourism—a fact he wasn't about to let me forget, ever), but he looked no more than fifteen.

He wore flip-flop sandals, short shorts that rose uncomfortably high on his thighs, a Fidel Castro–style green hat cocked to the side, and a green tank top that read in English, "Ca$h Rules Everything."

He was about five foot six and 120 pounds. In addition to the initial shock that my boss was younger—and indeed *looked* so much younger—than I, his appearance startled me. Everything about him was grossly out of proportion.

His nose was enormous, and this is something I can say without feeling bad, because my own isn't exactly petite. His, though, was crooked, leaning to one side just enough to make me wonder if it caused him respiratory problems. His nostrils, however, had a permanent flare to them that must have made up for any inhalation deficiencies caused by the crookedness. His neck was too big for his head—like a wrestler's, but worse, since it wasn't balanced out by large muscles elsewhere on his body.

He had easily the largest Adam's apple I'd ever seen on a human being. It bobbed up and down enthusiastically, as if doing calisthenics, every time he spoke. And, because the picture just wouldn't have been complete without them, he had a set of pointy elfin ears shooting out from his head.

When he removed his Fidel hat, he revealed a glistening helmet of hair slicked back with ungodly amounts of gel into an aggressive faux hawk. His hair and ears formed three towering, sinister peaks that all seemed to point directly at me no matter where I stood—like the eyes of the Mona Lisa.

When he spoke, every vein in his neck bulged out, causing a disturbance that made it seem as though talking even at an indoor volume caused him pain. He would tilt his head at an angle and the rope-like veins and hyperactive Adam's apple caused a commotion. As for his voice, there may be an actual medical term for it, but the best I can do is say he sounded like Kermit the Frog. Along with the neck's peculiar components, it all combined for a perfect storm of verbal and physical cacophony.

His feet were also large—noticeably larger than mine—particularly the toes, which is not insignificant since I was about half a foot taller. But it was his hands that got me the most. They were fit for a man twice his size. They were absolutely massive. Really—I can't stress enough how truly gigantic and out of place his hands were. They were so disproportionately large for his body that, after a while, they were all I could look at. On top of their excessive size, he used them—in conjunction with his permanently puckered lips—in a manner that can only be described as effeminate. They were giant ogres of hands that moved daintily through the air and into pockets and across cell phone keypads as if they were scared of injuring the air around them.

The combination of all this would horrify me for weeks to come.

This was my boss. His name was Juan Mendoza.

JUAN AND I MET IN the city of Chone, a place that—true to description—could have been one of those dusty old Western towns where the music stops when a stranger walks into the saloon. To get to where I was going to live, we hopped on a bus that took us about twenty-five minutes outside the city.

. We got off and walked down a long driveway with rice fields on either side. It belonged to Juan's family—a family that I would soon discover *was* this town. The Peace Corps information sheet I received for La Segua listed the population at a few hundred. It was actually quite a bit less than that where I lived because the documented figure included several surrounding communities. A more conservative estimate, according to the president of the community (a man who walked around barefoot and shirtless, even at town meetings) was 150. But still, it never felt like it, since everyone lived in small houses separated by acres of farmland.

The Mendoza family owned the majority of this land, which began as one giant farm that got divided up as the offspring multiplied.

The farm I would live on was the original property settled by the now-deceased patriarch of the family who guaranteed future Mendoza dominance of the area by siring about twenty children with the same woman. About a dozen of these Mendozas, now ranging from their early thirties to late fifties, stuck around the area and spawned on average three kids each. So to say the Mendozas dominated the La Segua population is no exaggeration.

A hundred yards to the right of the farm sat a wooden house belonging to Juan's uncle Homero, one of the many Mendoza brothers. To the left, at the end of the long mud driveway, was my new residence—an imposing three-story cinder-block structure surrounded by trash and chickens. Because the gaggle of aunts who worked around the clock in the second-story kitchen constantly dumped dirty water out the open windows, the swampy stench of moist chicken shit cocooned the house.

Juan walked me inside and began the not-so-easy task of introducing me to the Mendozas. It became clear that the answers he provided on my Peace Corps information sheet turned out to be half-truths that went well beyond just the town population. It said four other humans lived in the house I would sleep in. When I arrived, the actual figure hovered between a dozen and fifteen. I got the feeling there would be more, not fewer, as time went by.

There was the Mendoza family matriarch who was still going strong after spending the equivalent of fifteen years of her life pregnant. There were two of her daughters, who each had four toddlers. One of them also had a teenage girl with breasts so painfully enormous it'd be impossible not to mention them. There was another toddler in the mix and to this day I'm not sure whom he belonged to. And of course, there was Juan, who had moved into this same house—against Peace Corps regulations and the wishes of his extended family. His parents had their own farm in a nearby town but he apparently preferred it here.

Last but not least, there was a young mentally handicapped kid named Benicio. He wasn't related to the Mendoza family and his origins only grew more mysterious to me over time. His main purpose around the house, it seemed, was to do chores. At first I found this endearing, until I realized that the family treated him more like an indentured servant. When I first met him, he seemed overly excited and stared at me—sometimes with intense curiosity, other times like he wanted to kill me. It took me a couple of weeks to figure out which room he slept in, a fact that was particularly disquieting because late at night, he took to hiding in dark corners of the house then popping out of the shadows as I passed by, scaring the living shit out of me. The first few times he did this, I nearly knocked him out cold out of reflex. Later my nerves calmed and it merely gave me the creeps.

When Benicio wasn't stalking me, he continued doing chores around the house while dozens of Mendozas screamed at him. One night, when the grandmother was descaling fish in the kitchen, he crouched down and hit her legs with a cloth to keep the mosquitoes away; it reminded me of how farm animals line up and whip their tails to keep flies off one another.

Juan took me to the bottom floor to show me the room I'd be living in—a ten-by-fifteen-foot space enclosed by dungeon-like brick walls. The only window looked out to one of the puddles of chicken shit. The door was made from scrap plywood; it still had the spray-paint markings on it from the delivery crate it was pried from. I could have punched through it.

Juan iterated that this was the room that Pilar, Peace Corps Ecuador's head of Safety and Security, had approved when she'd made a site-inspection visit months earlier.

"See," Juan pointed, "we put netting over that window because she asked."

He was right—no mosquitoes flew through the net he'd glued over the window; instead, they visibly swarmed through the ceiling gap between floors just a few feet away.

We turned around and Juan took me down the hall to the bathroom. It was a three-by-three-foot concrete basin with a bowl of water for pouring over yourself. There was no sink or running water.

If I needed a toilet, I had to use the outhouse. It was behind the house, through a maze of chickens, pigs, and used diapers strewn from the second-story windows. Between the hornet nest and the cockroaches and the spiders, the outhouse indeed scared the shit out of me. In addition to the other obstacles between the front door and outhouse, I had to cross through a labyrinth of barbed-wire clotheslines. The wire was at just above head level of my Ecuadorian housemates, meaning it was right at decapitation height for me if I wasn't careful.

All of this—the room, the outhouse—excited me in a way. *If it weren't so dreadful*, I thought, *it wouldn't feel like the Peace Corps.*

Back inside, Juan handed me a lock for the plywood door that had the weight and girth of one normally used for luggage. He said good night. I crawled under the mosquito net, dripping in sweat, and read a biography of Jim Morrison by the light of my headlamp.

At about 5 a.m., I heard Juan pawing at the door. He wanted to take me out onto the wetland and see what we'd be transforming into an ecotourism paradise during my two years. The wetland was just on the other side of the road from the Mendoza farm. It was the only road in La Segua and doubled as a highway connecting the major inland city of Santo Domingo to the coastline. Every so often, amid the cow herds, snakes, and school children on rusty bicycles, a bus would speed through town at seventy miles an hour, kicking up a cloud of dust that barely settled before the next one screamed past. At the first and only town meeting I ever attended, one parent stood up and suggested they buy concrete mix and lay down a few extra speed bumps on the mile of road stretching through La Segua.

"Our kids are in danger," he shouted above a crowd that was murmuring disapproval. "I'll buy the concrete myself if it makes our kids safer." Others in the room shouted him down. Another person said, "Yeah, but then we'd have to slow down our trucks every time we pass over the bumps." (The word they used for speed bump, *chapa muerto*, translated to "dead cop.")

This morning, Juan and I crossed the highway, ducked under a barbed-wire fence, then walked another hundred yards through tall dry grass toward the water. The entire time, he explained his vision for the wetland. He had already secured funding from the United States Agency for International Development, or USAID. He was quite proud of this, despite having no idea that USAID was associated with the U.S. government. It actually took me several minutes to figure out what he was talking about because acronyms are customarily sounded out in the Spanish language, so he was referring to it as *ooh-sigh-eed*.

In short, he wanted to get a long dock built, extending from the road out to the water, complemented by a three-story bird-watching tower. He wanted several canoes to take the tourists around the lake. He kept referring to "the tourists" as if they were some giant, all-powerful, all-knowing bloc of white people who would come en masse to spend money there. A couple of times, he referred to them as "your people."

"Then the tourists will walk down this way, following me," he would say, or "Then the tourists will stand here and listen to me . . ." It always ended with said tourists handing over money to Juan and heading on their merry way. For the most part, he had a point: White people from rich countries do like to spend lots of money to visit poorer countries, where they stare at things and climb to the tops of places and wear fanny packs and overpay for stuff, and then return home and tell all their friends so they can do the same. I've been to many of those places.

But this was not one of them.

The wetland was indeed beautiful. There were birds (Juan's uncles used to shoot them) and fish (Juan could tell you exactly how many species) and the biggest iguanas I'd ever seen (Juan said they're delicious). The water was shallow and calm, and the scene of the wetland in the early mornings when fishermen were out with their nets was tailor-made for those coffee-table books of gritty, yet beautiful images of South America. But as a tourist attraction, it was underwhelming. No one would fly all the way down to Ecuador just to see it. I'm not sure what the hell else I was expecting to find. I was a volunteer, and this was what I was there to do.

Juan, in his cartoonish voice, began rattling off facts about the area, which sometime in the last decade they'd—quite wisely—gone from calling a "swamp" to a "wetland."

Fact: At an international conference on wetlands in Iraq some years earlier, this—*our*—wetland, Humedal La Segua, was included, making it one of the top 4,000 wetlands in the world.

Fact: Raúl Sanchez, their connection to USAID, had worked in the United States and spoke English. This made him somewhat of a deity figure in the world of ecotourism and grant siphoning.

Fact: This wetland—all of it—belonged to his family, meaning it was no problem whatsoever that it was being usurped for ecotourism purposes.

This last fact turned out to be not much of a fact at all. You might even categorize it as a lie, given that it was completely false. The truth would reveal itself with time.

For now, I was the first of what they fantasized would be many gringos to be canoed around the waters by a certified ecotourism guide of Humedal La Segua. Juan continued to point out different sights with his ginormous hands and then turn to me, eyes bulging, with a look that said, *Did you get a load of that? Huh?*

It all seemed so easy the way he explained it that I wondered for a moment why they even needed a Peace Corps volunteer. They would build a little of this infrastructure stuff, tourists would migrate in, and the financial windfall would heal all the economic and social woes of the surrounding town. This latter point was sold heavily on his application materials to the Peace Corps.

The rest of my short visit was mostly gringo show-and-tell with various other people around town. On my second evening there, an uncle of Juan's invited us into the back of his pickup truck for a "short ride" to his farm and back. More than an hour passed and we were still in the truck, driving down a dirt road in the dark at what felt like ninety miles an hour while I ducked my head to dodge overhanging tree limbs. The uncle at one point asked me if I wanted to drive. I said I didn't know how to drive a stick shift; plus, I said, it was against Peace Corps rules. A smile crept to his face as he said, "There are no rules here."

Later that same night, Juan and I were invited to dinner at his uncle Roger's home. The house perched on stilts halfway out into the wetland. When we arrived, Roger's wife, Veronica, suggested to me that we "get dinner." I agreed. She led me out the front door and down the ladder where she picked up a live chicken and handed me a machete. "Kill it," she said. I stalled for a bit with the machete in my hand. The aunt told me to stop being such a faggot, at which point I realized I'd eaten tons of chicken in my life and had no business eating it if I couldn't kill it myself. I sliced the chicken's throat with the machete and we ate it an hour later.

On the final night of my visit, Juan and I walked a mile down the road to eat at a neighbor's house. This neighbor, a mother of two in her early thirties, was the oldest in Juan's group of ecotourism guides. She gave me some hope that the show wasn't just being run by kids. We drank freshly squeezed orange juice and ate crackers.

In the background, a grainy TV played the nightly Ecuadorian news.

"Ah, President Correa," I said. "You guys fans?"

"Oh yes, he's the best," they both said, nearly in unison.

"What about you?" Juan said. "Do you like him?"

I smiled. "Well, a few days ago, a group of us were in Quito down around the main square, and the president drove by hanging his head out the window and he saw me and a friend of mine standing there. He yelled, 'Where are you from?' So I yelled back, 'Los Estados Unidos!' and he gave me the thumbs up. It was the first time I'd ever spoken to any president, now that I think about it. So I guess I like him."

They stared blankly.

"What about your president?" said Juan. "What's your opinion of . . . what's his name—?"

"Obama. Barack Obama."

"Yes, Barack Obama," he said, pronouncing it unrecognizably.

"Well, we're not allowed to express political opinions at all, so—"

"Oh, don't worry," he said. "You can say anything in front of us. We work together now, so it's, you know, total trust."

"Right. Well I voted for him, but we'll see. It's a little too soon to start saying whether I think he's a good president."

They both nodded in satisfaction with my answer. On the television, there was a story about a protest of sorts involving people in the sierra, near Quito. Seeing it, Juan launched into a monologue on how terrible the people from the sierra were. There are, you know, more indigenous people up there, he said. The *serranos* with all their greed and sneaky ways were the reason people like him and his community on the coast were poor.

I nodded.

His monologue wound down and he ended it with, "At least there's no racism in this country. Zero. The U.S., you know, is very racist. Very."

"How do you know?" I said.

"It is. It just is. You know. We've seen the pictures."

Yes, there's racism in the United States—there is everywhere—but I decided I'd defend my country against someone who'd never left the town he was born in.

"You know we just elected a black president, right?" I said. The fact that Obama is half-white was a detail I'd skip in this conversation.

"Obama is black?" he said.

"Yeah, have you seen any pictures of him on the news or anything?"

"Yes, sure. Obviously," he said.

"So then you already knew that he's black."

We looked at each other.

"What's your point?" he finally said.

"If our country just elected a black person, we can't be *that* racist, right?"

He stared at me blankly.

"Okay, never mind."

I woke up early the next morning hoping to get into Chone in time to connect to a bus leaving for Quito by 7 a.m. From Chone, it would be a six- or seven-hour ride to Quito (and then another two from there to Cayambe, and yet another hour from Cayambe to Olmedo). When I told Juan 7 a.m., he thought I meant 9 a.m., so I got off to a late start, since he insisted on taking the bus with me into Chone. Soon we gave up on waiting for a bus in La Segua and hitched a ride in the back of a pickup. At the Chone terminal I got on a bus headed for Quito.

Everything was normal inside the air-conditioned bus except for two things: The *ayudante*, or bus steward, seemed to be in an especially foul mood, and the bathroom in the back of the bus, near where I was sitting, had a sign on the door saying it was for women and for urination only. Early into the ride I noticed that when women went to the bathroom, the *ayudante* would stand right outside the door. When they finished and walked out, he immediately stepped in the lavatory and inspected it.

When we stopped for lunch an hour later, I made sure to force out a piss so I wouldn't have to break the rules. I grabbed some yogurt, a bag of chips, and a soda, and got back on the bus. About an hour after that, just after we passed through Santo Domingo, a churning pain seized my midsection. A hurricane was brewing in my bowels. It hurt so bad I couldn't hold it in. I was about to experience the hottest and heaviest case of the runs of my life and there was nothing I could do about it.

The bus was winding up into the cloud forest, through what is widely considered the most dangerous road in the country, climbing roughly 9,000 feet of the elevation between the coast and Quito in a series of sharp turns. I stood up, hunched over from the pain, and walked a few rows back to the bathroom door. It was locked. I shook it and rattled it and banged it until a little kid a few rows up saw me and wagged his finger. "You have to go up to the front and ask the *ayudante* to open it for you," he said.

I walked to the front, still hunched over and bumping into every seat on the way, and asked the ill-tempered *ayudante* if I could use the facilities. He asked why the hell I didn't use the bathroom back at the pit stop. I looked him in the eye and just said, "It's an emergency." I don't know if it was the urgency in my voice or the fact that I was now sweating bullets, but he pitied me and led me back to the female-urination-only bathroom, where once inside, I could barely drop my drawers fast enough before my ass exploded into a dark Jackson Pollock all over the metallic airplane-style toilet bowl. The stench was so foul I pried open a window that was partially welded shut to get some fresh air.

The sweating subsided and the feeling of relief was almost orgasmic. I looked to my left and found that the toilet paper dispenser was . . . empty. The thought of a very squishy four more hours on the bus crossed my mind, so I started searching frantically all over the place. Nothing. Back pockets? Nothing. Left pocket? Just my ID and ATM card. No. Right pocket? Something felt like paper. I pulled it out. It was not paper. It was an old one-dollar bill, filthy to the point that it was no longer green—so flimsy you could have blown your nose into it. I unfolded the bill and apologized to George Washington.

I walked out of the lavatory and returned to my seat. Either the *ayudante* knew what was going on in there or he got hit with my aroma right when I exited. Whichever the case, he didn't have the nerve to go in and inspect after I was done.

I soon fell into a minor panic thinking that with the dollar-bill wipe, I had risked an exposure to hepatitis or something as serious, but my nerves calmed when I remembered that in our first week there, we got hit with what seemed like a dozen shots and vaccinations. (In fact, I'm pretty sure I was *over*-vaccinated for Hep A because the doctors were pumping me with another dose every time I saw them—despite my protests that I'd been to Africa and done it all before.)

Later in the ride, I had to pee badly, but feeling I'd already pressed my luck with the bathroom facilities, I aimed into an empty 7Up bottle. It promptly gushed up over the opening like a geyser and overflowed into my lap.

CHAPTER 9

The last half of training was a downer. By then, all the trainees had formed high-schoolish cliques with the others whose sites would be nearby. This put me in an awkward position because no one would be sharing my site or living very close to La Segua.

Our last big hurrah in training was our technical trip—basically a field trip for all the staff and trainees to a resort in the cloud forest a few hours west of Quito. In the mornings, we went to an "integrated farm" and, in small groups moving around from station to station, received speed lessons on things like digging irrigation ditches and cultivating tilapia farms.

One afternoon, we gathered for a special session conducted by an American psychologist, or Larry the Therapist—an older guy with a thick northeastern accent. He showed up with his wife, who wasn't a therapist but sat barefoot on the floor in loose-fitting yoga pants while Larry did the talking.

I admit I was excited. I thought we all could benefit from some group therapy and was interested to see what direction it took.

Larry the Therapist introduced himself and his wife and told us all about their lives there in Ecuador and how great it was to be semiretired, living in the tropics, enjoying the occasional therapeutic seminar for great organizations like the United States Peace Corps, and basically how absolutely fantastic it was to be Larry the Therapist.

And since we were already there—also sitting on the floor barefooted, while Larry sat high in a chair looking out over us—he thought he might as well tell us about the beautiful son he and his wife had raised and how that son was now facing the terrors of indecision over whether to attend law school at NYU or the University of Michigan.

Larry the Therapist's wife interrupted him midsentence several times, once to share an anecdote about their dog eating the next-door neighbor's chicken. Larry got back on track to finish, saying that he was sure his son would make the right decision by "listening to the voice inside his head." And that, he said, was what we volunteers should do during our once-in-a-lifetime experience in Ecuador—we should "listen to the voice inside our head, because it's usually right."

Larry the Therapist's session came to a climax with an activity in which we broke up into pairs and talked about our reasons for joining the Peace Corps. The goal of the activity, said Larry, was not to just listen but to *actually listen*. He pointed out—and I couldn't have agreed more—that most of the time when we listen to someone talk, we're not really listening at all to the actual words, but thinking instead about other things, like what we're going to say next.

We went around the room one at a time and shared the answer our partner had given. One of the two married men in the group joked that he was there because his wife had made him. Everyone laughed except the wife. (They ended up quitting after seven weeks in site.)

Larry announced that we'd run out of time, and the session broke up.

That night after dinner we had a talent show and I played Bob Dylan's "It's All Over Now, Baby Blue" on the guitar.

IN THE WANING DAYS OF training, we came across so many new acronyms and manuals that we needed *other* acronyms and manuals to explain what was going on in the original ones. Several training sessions were dedicated to introducing CAT, or Community Assessment Tools. It was a project we needed to complete in our first few months at site. We would have to interview every household in our village to see what the community had (or lacked) in terms of resources. Busy work, said some; essential for community integration, said others. After putting it together, we were supposed to present our findings, preferably in a PowerPoint presentation, at a conference of volunteers and counterparts five months hence. Even though we had already been assigned to communities with counterparts who had requested us for specific jobs, this was aimed toward helping us figure out what other projects we could do. I imagined how strange a "needs assessment" was going to look in my community, where people lacked running water but had TV sets and cell phones that played MP3s.

All of this was explained in a PowerPoint presentation that demonstrated what our own PowerPoint presentations should resemble. In conclusion, said the program officer, CAT was designed to give us "structure in an unstructured environment."

We were told about our quarterly VRFs, or Volunteer Report Files, which tracked the progress of our program objectives. We spent more time being taught how to log in and fill out the Excel spreadsheet for our VRFs than we did learning about compost the day we took a field trip to the integrated farm.

If any of us failed to remember that this was the twenty-first century Peace Corps, we were sadly mistaken.

I also spent those final weeks of training living in utter fear of the medical office. A young woman in our training group I'd made friends with was abruptly kicked out when Nurse Nancy discovered that she had been taking an antianxiety medication the Peace Corps didn't know about. My friend had told the Peace Corps—during the same hellish medical clearance process I navigated—that she used to take the drug; she just hadn't told them she was now back on it. She divulged this offhand during the same type of meet-and-greet that I'd had with Nurse Nancy. When the medical staff found out about it, my friend was sent home less than forty-eight hours later.

I lived in fear just thinking about all the things in my medical past that the Peace Corps didn't know about. I was in a serious car accident when I was five years old that resulted in temporary paralysis, brain surgery, a skin graft, a broken jaw, and broken collarbones—among other bumps and bruises—but I hadn't listed any of this stuff for the Peace Corps since all their questions asked for *recent* history. I felt nervous that something would come up, or that they'd spot one of my scars, and it was only a matter of time before I, too, was out of there.

CHAPTER 10

Training ended and our swearing-in ceremony took place at the U.S. ambassador's residence in Quito. The ambassador, country director, and the training manager all gave speeches. We raised our right hands and swore an oath. Then, a fellow volunteer from our training group—Inner Peace Mark—walked to the podium and spoke. The theme of his speech was "heroes." He said we volunteers were *all* heroes. As he said the word "heroes," he paused, lifted his head, and scanned the room, looking at each one of us and nodding.

Heroes.

That night, we threw a party at a bar in a trendy Quito neighborhood and everyone got stumbling drunk. Several volunteers who'd been in the country for a while came into town just for the party. One of them walked around the dance floor selling pot out of a fanny pack. Later on, a married woman said she'd had dreams about having sex with me and asked me to make out with her. She tried to crawl on top of me while I lay in a beanbag chair in a room full of neon lights. I said no, thank you. Her husband was sitting five feet away smoking a cigarette and rolling his eyes like it wasn't the first time it had happened.

In the morning I peeled myself out of bed and took a taxi to the south Quito bus station. The long dark corridor of ticket windows was filled with men screaming names of cities so intensely that you'd think they were trying to talk you out of your intended destination and into going to theirs instead.

I was on my bus for less than an hour when I got a call from my program manager.

"Hi, uh, this is Winkler. What are you doing?" he said.

"I'm on the bus out to my site."

"Do you, uh, have a minute?"

"Yes." We were weaving back down the same treacherous road that I'd been heading up when I had my intestinal explosion.

He began reading from a script illustrating the horrors of the swine flu virus and then rattled off a bunch of ways to avoid too much contact and germs. Keep a week's worth of food stockpiled at your home, he said. And don't tell anybody in your community that you have the bird flu vaccine in your medical kit.

"You got all that?" he said.

"Yes, thank you."

"Goodbye."

When we were an hour outside Chone, the bus driver tried to pass by a tiny white coupe brimming with six or seven people where the road made a blind curve leftward around a small hill. When he thought he'd gone past, he let the bus swing back wide to the right, crashing into the coupe and tossing it against the road barrier. The jolt came from right outside my window. I looked down and saw broken glass and mirrors and mangled doors hanging open.

Our driver kept on going. He didn't even slow down. Minutes later, the banged-up coupe came roaring after us with pieces of metal dragging on the road, kicking up a wake of sparks behind it. When we reached a straightaway, the coupe pulled in front of the bus and slowed down to a stop, forcing us to pull over behind it.

The driver of the white coupe jumped out of his car, ran up to the bus, and started banging his fist on the door. All the passengers lurched to my side of the bus to see what was happening. The bus driver and his *ayudante* stepped down off the bus and got in a yelling match with the driver of the coupe, whose family was now standing behind him. He wore a white tank top that looked like it'd been stained with motor oil. He screamed and yelled while the women behind him wailed. He pointed to the damage on his car as the bus driver peeked at the side of the bus to see what damage he'd done to his own vehicle.

The yelling went on until it looked like they'd reached an agreement. Both men returned to their respective vehicles. The white coupe followed us all the way to Chone and into the bus station.

CHAPTER 11

We arrived just as the sun was going down. Juan was waiting
for me at the bus station with a few other certified ecotourism
guides. They greeted me and one offered to take my bag.

"Wow, that's really heavy," he said, trying to lift it.

"I'm going to be here for two years," I said.

"Oh, right."

"But I can carry it if it's too much."

He handed the bag back to me. Juan and I hitched a ride in the
back of a pickup heading out to La Segua and pulled into the long
driveway in the dark.

The population of my host family had grown to almost twenty
since my previous visit. One more of Juan's cousins—a single mother
of three in her late twenties named Sandra—was now living there.
She was pretty and kind and recently divorced.

And then there was Esteban, another of Juan's relatives, a slightly
cross-eyed guy in his midthirties who had a big potbelly. Juan referred
to him as an uncle, but based on my understanding of the family tree,
he was actually a second cousin. I could describe this man in several
ways, but the day I met him I wrote down one word about him in my
notebook and underlined it: dangerous.

The room next to mine on the bottom floor now belonged to a
man in his eighties who wasn't related to the family and never spoke a

word to me. No one ever gave me a straight answer on who he was or why he was there. He had old, leathery skin and walked around muttering to himself. Whenever he saw me, he waved his hands around in an odd, made-up sign language.

That first night I dragged my two duffel bags into my room and began to settle in. Right away in my dungeon-like quarters, I was jockeying for real estate with spiders, moths, and cockroaches. Within the first week, I reached my breaking point and bought some chemicals to smoke out the critters.

Before heading to the outhouse one night, I sprayed down the room with the bug spray and turned on my fan to create a cyclone of toxic air while I left. When I returned and opened the door, I was hit by an exodus of bugs toward the threshold, like when pepper spray hits a group of rioters and they scramble for the exits. The fumes from the spray were so bad I sat wearing the face mask from my medical kit as I wrote in my journal.

At night I could hear rats crawling above me in the rafters. During breakfast the next morning I mentioned the rats, and Esteban flashed me a smile, exposing several missing teeth and a lazy eye. He was overjoyed to help me with my problem.

That afternoon, he came back to the house with a box of rat poison, complete with a skull-and-crossbones warning label. He got up on a ladder and scattered the pellets about. And then we waited.

During the night, I was awakened by the sound of rats asphyxiating and vomiting to death above my head. I would hear some raspy screeching sounds followed by a plopping noise. For several mornings after that, I'd get up and sweep dead rats that had fallen from the rafters out the front door. When the old man in the room next to mine saw me doing that, he used his sign language to insist that I leave the rats by the front door for him to take care of. He would scoop them up and walk off, muttering to himself.

CHAPTER 12

A s a survival mechanism, I constantly assessed the people I met and categorized them into two groups: those I could trust and those I couldn't.

One I trusted the most by far was Homero, the uncle who lived in the small house on the other side of the rice field. He wasn't the oldest of the army of Mendoza offspring, but he struck me as the most responsible. His young daughter acted like less of an animal than the other third-generation Mendozas wreaking havoc on the farm. Even more amazing, I suppose, was that Homero had just *one* child.

Since Esteban had begun answering every question I directed his way with "I kill gringos for fun," it was a relief to swing in a hammock in the afternoons and talk with Homero. He was legitimately interested in my life and the first person I met in La Segua who caught onto the fact that what I was doing was hard. On Sundays, he drove me in his giant yellow pickup truck—which required a hot-wiring maneuver every time it was started up—down to the far end of town to watch local soccer games and drink beer. After a few beers he would start asking if I wanted to go to the whorehouse with him, and when I said no, he'd call me a faggot.

His pickup truck didn't have a functioning radio, so he sang to himself while driving. He was a really big fan of Queen and often launched into a long monologue about Freddie Mercury.

"Unbelievable!" he said. "All that talent and fame and money. He could have fucked any woman in the world but instead he decides he wants to be a faggot. Too bad." Homero just shook his head saying what a shame it was. Before long he'd resume singing in broken English: "I just want to be free!"

In the mornings, Homero walked across the field between the houses, sort of strutting with his potbelly wagging side to side underneath his tank top, and join us for breakfast. In earshot of his old and feeble mother, he'd end nearly every meal by saying, "Come on, let's go to the whorehouse." If he didn't attack my heterosexual bona fides, he just tsked and shook his head like I was making some grave error. Following maybe the twentieth invite and refusal, I asked, "Aren't you afraid of getting diseases or anything like that?" After several weeks in La Segua and about a hundred conversations just like this, his answer truly stunned me.

"That's what condoms are for," he said.

A CHARACTER WHO WAS ALWAYS teetering on the brink of trustworthiness was Homero's younger brother, Roger, whom I'd decapitated a chicken and dined with during my site visit. I learned very quickly that he was fun and kind. In my first weeks in La Segua, he and his wife were exceedingly generous in always inviting me over to their house and cooking me dinner. In typical coastal style, he, too, would hike his shirt up high on his chest, exposing a giant round gut. We always joked that he was eight months pregnant. He loved the Discovery Channel, which was one of the two or three channels people in the area could pick up through their antenna. The result was an impressive ability to transition between asking me if the United States was in Europe and then saying something like, "Did you know dolphins are the smartest mammal on earth?" Roger was also a good fisherman and recovering alcoholic. And he was—even by Ecuadorian standards—a chronic adulterer.

One day at breakfast, I bargained Homero down from a trip to the whorehouse to a trip out on the wetland with him and his fisherman buddies. Roger was included in the group. I jumped at the chance for a bonding experience that involved zero risk of venereal disease. It was a good way to really get to know the community I was supposed to be a part of—not to mention the wetland. Also, this was during a time when Juan had disappeared for about a week straight without telling me how long he'd be away or where he'd be.

Out on the water after the sun had just come up, I looked around at the foothills in the distance and had a profound sense of joy that this was the gritty land down south I had come here for. It was actually one of the first times in Ecuador that I felt like I was in the Latin America I'd always envisioned. For the month at site leading up to this, I was feeling as though I'd entered a very dark and disturbing place where people spoke nearly unintelligible Spanish and treated me like an incompetent. Those first weeks felt like a vacation mixed with a nightmare—and the two were blending together to the point where I couldn't tell the difference.

After my transcendent gaze in the distance, I looked at my immediate surroundings and saw a group of about eight fishermen of varying ages strip down to their tighty whities and proceed to play grab-ass while making jokes about one another's mothers and calling each other faggots. In a bathing suit and T-shirt, I was unprepared for my morning out on the water and would earn a gruesome sunburn.

I teamed up with Roger and we swam around the shallow water, setting up traps for shrimp after we'd helped with the big fishing nets. When it was just the two of us, we talked about all sorts of things. He, too, was disappointed about my lack of appetite for whorehouses. I asked him if he indulged and he said yes, "But only to drink beers." Right. For coastal men whose wives had them on a short leash, this was their "I only read *Playboy* for the articles" denial of participation. With the intimidating way his wife, Veronica, forced me to murder that chicken back in May, I got the idea that she didn't take much shit from her husband.

Roger told me that one of his three children was actually Veronica's daughter from a previous marriage. His kids were eleven, nine, and seven years old. I asked him if he had kids from another marriage.

"I was never married before Veronica, but I had kids with another woman," he said.

"And those kids live with the other woman?"

"Yeah, she lives further down the road toward Chone."

"Oh, how old are those kids now?" I asked.

"One of them is seven and the other is one and a half."

"Okay," I said. As we were swimming through the water carrying the shrimp baskets with the sun beating down on us, I thought for a moment about the ages of those kids.

"Roger," I said. "I don't understand."

"What?"

"How are your kids with the other woman younger than your kids with Veronica?"

A sheepish little smile appeared on his face. "That other woman was a girlfriend. Kind of a fling," he said, nodding his head as if we now had an understanding.

"Veronica must have been really upset . . ."

"Yeah, she was fucking pissed," said Roger.

Then I thought about it even more. "Wait a second, Roger—you had a baby with this woman seven years ago—"

"Yup."

"—and Veronica got really mad—"

"Uh-huh."

"And then five years later—two years ago—you have another baby with her."

"Yeah." He grinned.

"Holy shit, Roger! What did Veronica say the second time?"

"She was even madder. You know, just really mad. But it's fine because I told her I was done with the other woman."

"All done?" I suddenly felt like I was the thirty-three-year-old father and he was the twenty-three-year-old kid.

"Yeah, yeah. It's all done," said Roger.

We swam on. He asked me more about my family, about my sex life, about life in general. We caught more shrimp. I could feel my neck and arms getting more and more dangerously sunburned. And we swam some more.

Several days later, Roger was supposed to be at our house at 9 a.m. so we could drive to another town and have a barbeque. At noon, when he still hadn't arrived, I went over to Homero's house to lie in a hammock and do a crossword puzzle. Homero's two-story farm-house had turned into the only place where I could escape the zoo of screaming kids and get some peace and quiet. While I lay there swinging, I asked Homero if he knew why Roger hadn't shown up.

"He had a bad night," he said.

"What happened?"

"He's in trouble with Veronica." I stared at him as if to say, *You've gotta be kidding me.* "He was hanging out with a woman that lives up that way. Do you know about that woman?"

"Yeah, he's told me all about her."

"Well, he was with that woman last night and Veronica found out."

"Oh Jesus," I said. "I thought by now—"

"He never learns."

Soon Roger and Veronica showed up. She was in a bad mood. She came toward me with a machete in her hand. I put down the cross-word puzzle book, jumped up, and backed away. I couldn't really tell if she was joking but didn't want to take any chances. She was talking too fast for me to understand but I still got the message. What I could decipher was that Roger's alibi for last night's shenanigans was that he was out drinking with me. He'd dragged me into his world of lies and now I was facing the business end of a machete.

Veronica eventually put down the machete—it turns out she was only half serious—and we all left for the barbeque. After that, I never turned my back on Veronica, or the rest of them.

Later on at the barbeque, I pulled Roger aside and told him to stop it with the other woman—or at least not drag me into it. I suggested it in the best way you can to someone a decade older than you. He told me not to worry—he had already cut it off for good.

"When did you cut if off?" I asked.

"Oh . . . later."

The next time I was over at Roger's house, I think he felt guilty about all this and had an impromptu heart-to-heart with me. It was right after he'd shown me a boa constrictor he found snared in his fishing net that morning. He now had it trapped in one of his shrimp baskets and was periodically taunting it with sticks. We walked on the trail that led from the fishing boats back to his house when he started talking in-depth about his past and all the drinking and whoring.

It was pretty run-of-the-mill, woe-is-me stuff until he revealed to me that it wasn't just the drinking. He'd also been smoking weed every day.

"Well, that's not so bad," I said. "People can still function while doing that from time to time."

"Yeah, but I was sprinkling an entire vial of crack on top before I smoked it—and, you know, I was pretty much smoking it non-stop . . . all day, every day."

"That sounds pretty intense," I said.

"It was pretty bad. Pretty bad." He nodded his head and looked off into the distance. "But then I found Jesus, and he's all I need."

ANOTHER PERSON I CAME TO trust was Sandra, the cousin divorcee who was one of the newest additions to the house. It was her nightmarish trio of kids who made my life most miserable, but Sandra chose to take me under her wing when it came to things that everyone assumed I was incapable of. Chief among these tasks was laundry.

On weekend mornings, all the women of the house went out back, between the pigsty and the outhouse, under the barbed-wire clothes hanging area, and washed piles of clothes by hand using large tubs. For most men in my community, to be seen doing the laundry would have had emasculating repercussions, but I didn't have a wife to do it for me. So I joined the women out back.

Washing the clothes was easy and self-explanatory, but in an attempt to hold some sort of rank over me, the women constantly pointed out ways I was doing it wrong: I wasn't getting the water from the well correctly; I wasn't rinsing the clothes thoroughly enough; I was mixing incompatible colors, such as white and off-white. Sandra saw herself as my savior and offered a helping hand. I humored her. She enjoyed helping the poor gringo.

Doing our laundry side by side and talking became a tradition that I enjoyed. Sandra was a treasure trove of need-to-know information about our community. For instance:

A week before I came to town, a local girl was raped on the side of the road in broad daylight. This was one of the reasons the family I lived with forbade me from walking alone outside the property after nightfall. It was also why they got incredible looks of concern on their faces when I would leave to go jogging down the road in the mornings.

"Be careful," they said. "People will hurt you."

Also, since I'd arrived, there'd been a string of armed robberies at houses in La Segua. They took place farther down the road toward the coast—it was a distance of less than a mile, but the family talked about "farther down the road" like it was a different universe.

"Is this something we should be worried about?" I asked.

"No," said all the aunts. "This family has respect in this community, so no one would ever even try to come onto our property and hassle us."

Sandra told me that back in December, a few months before I arrived, they'd had a spree of gang-related broad-daylight murders in the streets of Chone. It got so bad that all bars had to close down for a few months. I'd talked about this with Juan, too. Even he was afraid to be outside after dark—in Chone or La Segua.

Was this something we should be worried about? I asked.

Again, the answer was no. Things had toned down since then.

Still, almost weekly we heard news of someone in a nearby community getting decapitated after a drunken argument and a machete fight. These stories, like the shootings, were verifiable in the local newspaper and usually the result of long-standing family rivalries or revenge for such high crimes as letting a cow wander onto someone else's property. Sandra talked about these other places like they were hell on earth; I'd been to a few of them around the outskirts of Chone, and they looked about the same as my community.

What it all amounted to was that people in the region seemed to be adept at living up to their reputation for barbaric violence. Back in training when I'd heard that this area was the "most dangerous part of the country," I thought it was more of a folkloric warning—the way people talk about the Old West. I assumed that stories about people resolving their conflicts with the same tools they used to clear brush was something that happened either back in the day or farther out in the boonies. Apparently this wasn't the case.

But apparently I had nothing to worry about.

Sandra also liked sharing general wisdom and life advice with me. She said I should find myself a woman there and stay forever. Then came the generic conversation about girlfriends I'd had in the past and the sexual habits of gringos. When I told her it's not unusual for gringos to have sex before marriage, she looked disgusted. "We—people here—don't have sex before marriage."

The following day, Sandra's unwed, pregnant sister arrived from out of town for an indefinite stay at our house. The pregnancy was seven or eight months along, and the sister had turned fifteen just a few months back.

CHAPTER 13

When Juan disappeared for days at a time, his departure was quick and mysterious. I'd wake up and he'd be gone without a trace. But when he was around, he was ubiquitous: He would ask me for money; knock on my door at 4:30 a.m. to ask if I could do his cousin's English homework (I told him not to knock that early again unless there was a life-threatening emergency); ask to borrow my camera indefinitely; stare at me without a word, nostrils flared and eyes glazed over, as I ate dinner; and watch me through my window while I slept as he "fed the chickens" at the crack of dawn (I caught him doing this several times).

After going away, he'd always reappear a few days later and announce that we had lots of work to do. Periodically, his group of guides would get together at the Mendoza house. Juan would do all the talking. Mostly the discussion revolved around setting the agenda for *other* meetings that would happen at an unspecified time in the future.

At the first official meeting of the Association of Ecotourism Guides of Humedal La Segua, I introduced myself and explained the role of the Peace Corps volunteer. I described that I'd be there for two years, that the Peace Corps' purpose was to do development projects in other parts of the world, and that it was also about a cultural exchange of sorts. I explained that as a natural resource conservation volunteer, I was to work with their group but also to find some community projects on the side. (I had actually given this little speech several times in Juan's presence, and every time I made the last point, he became visibly uncomfortable, the veins in his mammoth-sized neck bulging and his nostrils flaring more than usual.) I finished by telling them about the interviews I'd have to do for my Community Assessment Tools presentation. At that news, Juan began to squirm in his chair.

The other six guides said they were really happy to have me there. They appeared interested in where I was from and how I could help them. Besides Juan, who was president of the group—the "maximum authority," as he put it—there was Ignacio, the vice president. He was a classmate of Juan's at the university and also a recent recipient of a degree in tourism.

Ignacio and I got along. He was a workout enthusiast who, when he wasn't pumping iron, was cultivating an encyclopedic knowledge of Sylvester Stallone and Jean-Claude Van Damme films. When I'd see him for the first time in a day, he'd often greet me with a broken-English version of a signature line such as "I am the law." He would throw it out there in Spanish and then road test his elementary English. He was heartbroken to learn it'd been over a decade since I'd seen a movie starring either of his idols.

The guide named Carlos was about five foot five and 225 pounds, with a rat-tail hairdo crawling down his neck. He was a big fan of Bon Jovi. He was not, however, much of a fan of anything pertaining to the wetland. That, and his lack of a tourism degree—or any schooling beyond the fifth grade—made me wonder why he was in the group. He lived a short way down the road from the Mendoza farm and was always hanging around.

I recognized the thirtysomething woman I'd met briefly during my site visit, who was joined by another woman of about the same age from the next town down the road. She had a raspy voice and was always smiling.

There was also a man in his late twenties named Darwin (a

common name in Ecuador), who claimed to be a lawyer, but spent all day riding up and down the road on a child-sized bicycle.

The last member was a young guy whose name I could never remember. The first time I met him, Juan pulled me aside and warned me that he couldn't be trusted. I asked Juan for details and all he said was, "Look, he *can't* be trusted. There are certain things you can't say around him—I'll tell you about that later—but just remember not to trust him." Nevertheless, he was a fully registered and licensed ecotourism guide in Juan's association.

IN THOSE INITIAL WEEKS, I got dragged around, primarily between La Segua and Chone, for more "meetings." A lot of it was further gringo show-and-tell, but I didn't mind it much at first because it kept me busy. At the time, I occasionally got on the phone with other volunteer friends of mine and heard about how they were sitting inside all day reading books, dreading having to go outside—because of shyness or culture shock or the heat—and *do something* (such as their Community Assessment Tools interviews).

One night Juan and Ignacio informed me that the next morning we'd be taking a two-hour bus ride south to the provincial capital, Portoviejo, for a meeting at the government office of tourism. Ignacio pulled me aside as we were about to go home for the night. He had a somber look on his face.

"Grigsby, as you know, we're a new organization that is just beginning..."

"Yes," I said.

"And someday our group is going to have money—*a lot* of money. But right now we don't, so we were wondering if tomorrow you could pay for our bus fare."

"How much will it cost?"

"Umm, about $1.25 each way, so $2.50."

"So neither of you guys have $2.50?"

"Well, uh, you see, um, yeah, we do."

"You *do?*"

"Yes, we do. Of course we do!" he said. "Of course we have $2.50! What did you think?"

"Then why do you need me to pay for you if you have the money?"

He looked at me as if I was the one who just didn't understand.

"Okay," he said. "We have the money for the bus, but that's not it. Also, we'll need lunch when we get down there."

"All right, what's lunch, another $2.00?"

"Yeah."

"Sure, I'd be happy to help out, but you don't have another $2.00—$4.50 total?"

"No, I do—we both do. Of course we do," he said. His face twitched in what could have been a wink or a grimace.

"Then it sounds like you guys are all set."

"Oh yes, of course."

Portoviejo was another sweaty inland hell. The meeting turned out to be Juan printing a few pages of something off someone else's computer, signing it, and then handing it to a woman behind a desk. We also picked up some Department of Tourism materials like Galápagos postcards and free calendars. Before we left Portoviejo that afternoon, I went into a music store and spent eighty dollars on the only steel-stringed acoustic guitar I could find.

The one other time I saw Portoviejo was a few weeks later when we returned as part of a tourism expo. Groups of guides from different attractions in the coastal region had table displays showing off what their area had to offer, with fancy brochures and trinkets and posters. At our table, Juan's papier-mâché model of La Segua's wetland sat on a Styrofoam block. It was a little embarrassing, but when some fellow guides from different places informed us we could visit them for free in the future, Juan declared the day a success.

After a few consecutive weeks of nonstop meetings that weren't really meetings, I told Juan it might be more efficient if I spent some time introducing myself around the community and doing my interviews while he took care of his errands himself. I did the best I could to explain that most of his errands were "one-person jobs." I knew that by coming to a third-world country and talking about using time efficiently, I was fulfilling the most typical gringo stereotype. But an entire month of Juan wanting to be next to me at all times—insisting that he accompany me into Chone to buy toilet paper or demanding that I come to his university with him so he could get a document signed—was unbearable. He harrumphed and protested, saying that I *needed* to be everywhere he was because we represented the Association of Ecotourism Guides of Humedal La Segua together. But Juan eventually gave up and slunk away. It turned out to not matter, because soon after, he disappeared again.

I took the opportunity to get out in the community.

The predetermined Community Assessment Tool interview questions included all sorts of things, such as what conditions their houses were in, how many people were in the family, and what they did for a living. It also had questions about family income and local resources.

For the volunteers in our group more inclined toward conspiracy theories, this assignment set off some red flags, given that Ecuador was in the oil-rich Amazonian region that had been exploited for years by foreign companies. "Think about it," one volunteer said to me months later. "Our government is eventually collecting all these reports that include the vital statistics of these small communities that in some cases sit on top of extremely valuable resources." I suggested that if someone in the State Department was actually taking a look at CAT reports from Peace Corps volunteers in Ecuador, we had bigger problems to worry about.

I walked alone on the dusty road and knocked on doors to introduce myself. Generally, people were excited to talk to me. A lot of the time they were baffled by the questions, so I ultimately entered homes on the pretense of the interview but ended up just sitting down with them to explain who I was and why I was there. Some couldn't contain their awe at the prospect of an American coming to live in their community and work with them for a couple of years.

Once or twice, the people never invited me inside, and I stood on their doorstep asking the simple questions. Then they'd bark the question back to someone inside and wait for them to yell back the answer—even when I asked things like whether they had an indoor bathroom. At one house, I was so intimidated by the way a family looked at me as I stood at their door that I wrote down their names and ages, told them that was the entire interview, and left.

To most of the families, I described some of the projects I could get involved in—vague things about compost and fertilizers that I'd sort of learned during training. They nodded their heads enthusiastically. Next I'd mention that my primary job there was to work with the group of guides on the wetland, at which point people would clam up. Were they aware of who the group was and what it was doing? Sure, they nodded. But they would never say much about it.

I found out some interesting facts during my interviews: The wetland was actually divided up among fiftysome owners, the majority of whom were *not* Mendozas. And most of those landowners made up an organization—a cross between a cooperative and a homeowner's association—that got together to make decisions on matters pertaining to the wetland. Many of these people lived on the edge of the wetland and owned a section of land going into it, where they fished or set up a shrimpery. Others just lived somewhere between La Segua and Chone and owned a parcel of the wetland, either leasing it to fishermen or keeping it as a piece of real estate.

Also, a decade before, another group of guides had attempted to exploit the wetland for tourism. They had no success and dissolved.

Walking back along the highway in the pressing heat after a day of interviews, I experienced my first true bout of loneliness. It began in the pit of my stomach and reached out into the rest of my body. It felt as though the life had been sucked out of every one of my muscles. Everything seemed to be piling up: It was hot, it was dirty, and now even my internal organs felt lonesome. I went back to the house and sat in my room playing Johnny Cash and Van Morrison songs on my guitar.

✧ ✧ ✧

THE NEXT TIME I SAW Ignacio, I told him about my interviews and what I'd discovered about the co-op of landowners. "So there are all these plans to open up the wetland to tourism, but have any of you from the group of guides spoken with the head of their group?" I said.

"No, we don't need to," he said.

"That's not a little strange?"

"Strange how?"

"Maybe," I said, "it would help to coordinate with them in some way—to tell them what we'd like to do so they can help us and there's no confusion."

"Listen to me," he said. "Those people already have the land. They have everything they need. They have land and they have money." He made gestures with his arms out toward the wetland. We were standing in a cloud of dust waiting for a bus to come by. "So why would we have anything to do with them? No, no, no. Juan and I—we work for the people around here who don't have anything. They're the ones who need our help because they don't have land or anything like that."

"Oh."

"Now you see what I'm saying."

We both stared down the road in silence.

"Okay, so what's the plan to help these people you say need the help?" I asked.

"That's easy: When we get the tourism dollars, we'll do small projects for them here and there—gardens, things like that. You can help us with that," he said.

"Okay," I said.

Next I asked him about the other group of guides that had formed years back.

"Them? They failed," Ignacio said. "They didn't do anything right."

"What did people say? How come they fell apart?"

"They just didn't cooperate with anyone," said Ignacio. "They thought they could do it all on their own."

I nodded.

"That's why we—you know, we've studied this—and that's why we know how to do this the right way. And you will help us, of course."

"Let me ask you another question."

"Go ahead."

"What was the original reason you guys wanted a Peace Corps volunteer? I know all the stuff you wrote down on the application, like helping with community tourism projects and environmental education stuff, but what was the number one reason you decided to ask for a volunteer when you guys talked among yourselves—you and Juan and the group?"

He looked me in the eye and said matter-of-factly, "You're a gringo. You're white. You speak English." I nodded in understanding. "And, well, the type of tourists we hope to get here, they'll be white people who will speak English. So we wanted you here to be able to tell us the types of things that gringos like to see when they come to a place like this. And, of course, you can teach us English and things like that."

CHAPTER 14

The next week Juan drifted back to the Mendoza farm for the arrival of several hundred bamboo saplings that were to be planted in the wetland. It was part of a province-wide reforestation project, the details of which were fuzzy. This stretch of coast is terribly deforested because several decades back, the government actually encouraged it. In fact, they told people they could have large chunks of land for rock-bottom prices as long as they deforested the property. Clearly, the program was a rousing success: Large swaths of Manabí have been turned into scarred and barren tracts worthy of a *National Geographic* photo spread, but not in a good way.

A truck from the government office in Portoviejo dropped off the saplings in the shade of a tree along our driveway. Juan said he'd be off again—on this occasion to visit his parents' farm an hour away—and I promised to water the bamboo daily while he was gone.

The next time I was eating upstairs with Homero, I asked him about the bamboo that was going to be planted out in the wetland where he fished every day.

"Ha!" he chuckled. "Yes, that. I'm going to pull that bamboo out if it's planted."

"How come?"

"Oh man, you don't think any of that's going to work, do you?"

"Any of what?" I said.

"All that crap with the wetland—it's a crock of shit."

"Which part?"

"All of it, all of Juan's bullshit."

"Haven't you known about these plans for a while?" I said. "You agreed to it all, right?"

"Yeah, I did. Whatever. It's a crock of shit. Don't listen to my nephew. Hey, you wanna go to the whorehouse?"

Lately, Homero had been somewhat of a personal hero to me. On the floors above me, Sandra's pregnant fifteen-year-old sister had gotten her hands on a giant set of dance club–grade speakers and started blasting reggaeton music at a high volume. Reggaeton is a pitifully grinding genre that gained popularity briefly on the U.S. club-music scene in the mid-2000s only to be forgotten one or two hits later. Unfortunately, that popularity never waned in Ecuador. After the music blasted for about twelve hours straight two days in a row, Homero cut off the power to our house because the noise was bothering him and his family who lived the length of a football field away.

LATE ONE EVENING AROUND THIS time, I was in Chone and met a man named Roberto who owned a farm near my community. One of his parents was American and, decades before, he'd lived in the States for a year. He offered me a ride home in his truck.

As we rattled over potholes in the dark, I asked him if he had any advice on where I should look for a place to stay after my first few months. (It was a Peace Corps rule that we live with a host family for our first three months, after which we were free to find our own place, as long as the rent was less than seventy dollars a month.)

I think Roberto misunderstood me and instead jumped into general advice for living in my community. "The single most important thing to do," he said, "is to give the impression that you're someone who doesn't drink alcohol."

I just nodded and he kept speaking. "The people here, they seem nice, and some of them are. But when they drink, they turn into—how should I put it—ah, they turn into *animals*. Even the ones that aren't animals, they drink and when they drink they don't know when to stop and then they're, uh, dangerous. I don't know if you drink; when I was your age I drank, a lot. But don't drink with these people here. Drink all you want with a few of your friends, but the people here are not your friends." He dropped me off at the end of my driveway and told me to stop by his house anytime I wanted.

THAT SUNDAY, MY HOST FAMILY and I drove to a river nearby for lunch and some of the uncles began drinking beer. One of them turned into an animal.

While we were there, I managed some good conversation with other members of the family. I finally got around to talking to Sandra's fifteen-year-old sister, Evelyn, about her pregnancy. I'd been nervous about asking her for some time because, for one, seeing such a tiny young girl pregnant was a startling image, and second, I wasn't actually sure she was pregnant. All the women in her family seemed to have big midsections, so at first I wasn't completely positive. Then it was undeniable.

Sitting in the back seat of the pickup to stay out of the heat, I asked Evelyn where the father was.

"He died."

"Oh, I'm sorry to hear that. When?" I asked.

"Seven months ago."

I paused. "Can I go to the hospital when the baby comes?"

"Sure," she said.

We talked some more and she ran off to go swimming in the river while still wearing her jeans and T-shirt.

Another one of Sandra's sisters, Rosa, was in town for the weekend and joined us at the river. (Every time someone new showed up to the house, I was assured it was a temporary visit; the only time that was true, however, was with this third sister of Sandra's.) Rosa had her three-year-old boy with her.

Everyone else was down by the river, either swimming in full clothing with the women or aggressively drinking beer with the men.

I turned to Rosa. "Your little boy is really quiet, not like the others always crying and screaming and fighting. He's very calm," I said. After my interactions with the litter of other Mendoza kids, I felt this was by far the highest compliment I could have paid her.

"Yes, he's a quiet boy, but he's been more quiet lately since his dad died," said Rosa.

"My god. His dad—your husband—died? He's not living any longer?" I said. Since I'd become so accustomed to my host family telling me lies, later to be explained as "jokes," I had resorted to asking a question several different ways to sift out any misinterpretations.

"Yes, it's the truth. He died a month ago in an accident."

"What kind of accident?"

"An accident with a gun," she said.

"Was it his gun or someone else's?"

"His gun. We were outside doing work and we heard a big bang so I ran inside and I saw him lying dead on the floor," she said. "We don't know how it happened."

"I'm very sorry," I said. "Is it all hard to explain to your little boy? Sometimes these things are hard to explain to kids . . ."

"Yeah, it is. He sometimes asks where his daddy is, or when his daddy is going to come back home."

A few minutes later I said, "Wow, and Evelyn's baby's daddy died, too."

"No, no," she said. "He's alive."

I pressed her for more information. She said the father was a "bad person" who sold drugs and didn't want to be a part of the baby's life. In that earlier conversation with Evelyn, apparently she'd said her baby's daddy was "dead" in the way we might say he's "dead to me" (though giving a detailed description of the car accident that "killed" him, as she did, made for a pretty gruesome metaphor).

Back home that evening I asked Homero about the gun accident of his in-law.

"Accident? Ha! Yeah. Shit, that wasn't any accident. He took a gun and shot himself in the face like a coward."

"Did you know him well?"

"No. He was just a pussy, you know."

Homero seemed to be in an honest mood, so I asked him about the rape that happened down the road. He didn't know anything about it. I also asked him about the armed robberies.

"Yeah, yeah, yeah," he said. "Look, those families down that way, they don't have the respect around here that this family—my family—has. That kind of stuff would never happen to us. No one would ever come around here looking for trouble. No way. Nothing to worry about. Ha! Worry! Don't be a pussy."

CHAPTER 15

While Juan was away, I conducted a few more door-to-door interviews, but the heat and lethargic pace of life sapped most of the energy from my bones. I would wake up, do push-ups and sit-ups, finish a crossword puzzle, visit the outhouse, take a bucket bath in the cool well water, then walk upstairs for breakfast. This was all before seven o'clock. Then I'd retire to a hammock to blaze through more reading material. I'd finished a biography of baseball player Roberto Clemente and was on to *Undaunted Courage*, a story of the Lewis and Clark expedition.

At lunchtime, I sat and ate in the kitchen with all the aunts and uncles. The dangerous-looking one, Esteban, still hadn't gotten tired of the "I kill gringos" line, which to him remained laugh-out-loud funny. At the end of the meal, they got grave looks on their faces and asked why I would never finish my food. I explained that, for me, piping hot soup on a ninety-five-degree day didn't hit the spot. "You gringos are so strange," they'd say.

I was getting accustomed to eating while having a dozen or so people stare and critique my eating habits. But during one lunch of getting stared at, I let my pride get the best of me. It was the first time it happened in Ecuador. I was saying something and mispronounced the word "refrigerator." They all laughed.

"What is it?" I asked.

One of them told me I was saying it wrong. I tried to correct myself. I got it wrong again. They all roared in laughter once more, especially Sandra, who seemed to take a strange pride in the fact that my vocabulary had this giant shortcoming. Everyone else got over it and stopped laughing, but not Sandra.

"So then how am I supposed to pronounce it?" I said.

She laughed more and began pointing at me.

"Ooh! You don't know how to say it!" she whooped.

And so I said, "How many languages do you speak?"

IN THE AFTERNOONS I'D RETIRE to the hammock again, after having exhausted the realms of conversation with various family members. I could barely get through some of those days, even with an afternoon nap. Most nights I was getting close to ten hours of sleep, yet I still felt like I could return to bed immediately following breakfast. I was beginning to wonder if this was what serious malnutrition felt like. The plates they served me were heaping with food—a Chimborazo, they would call it, in reference to the country's highest volcano—and I would walk away from the table with my stomach aching it was so full. But since it was filled mostly with rice and other empty carbohydrates, I was starving forty-five minutes later.

During the time I was feeling so tired, one of the girls upstairs—Juan's eighteen-year-old cousin with the enormous-to-the-point-of-discomfort breasts who was always making eyes at me—came down with dengue fever. Already prone to hypochondria, I went into a tailspin with this news. First, I tried to convince the family not to toss the house's gray water outside from the second story. I explained that the moat of shallow standing water was a breeding fiesta for mosquitoes that bit us and transmitted things like dengue.

"But they don't bite us. They only bite you," they would say. "You're fresh blood."

I blew a hole through this theory by pointing out that it was one of their nieces, not me, who had dengue. I was trying to make sure no one else got it, I told them. Eventually I gave up. I gave up with this the same way I gave up trying to get them not to throw their trash and used diapers out the windows, creating a biohazardous wasteland between the back of the house and the berm leading down to the polluted Chone River. They laughed at me.

The mosquito business was particularly discomfiting for me since it meant I basically stayed indoors from dusk till dawn. Previously, I'd been trying to spend as much time as possible outdoors, especially in the late evening. The darkness inside my dungeon-like room heightened my loneliness. I spent long nights lying in that bed, sweating through the sheets under the mosquito net, thoughts ricocheting around in my head.

"What the fuck am I doing here?" I'd ask myself. "I'm surrounded by people I can't trust." I was worried about all the strange violence and afraid that I'd gotten myself trapped.

Life here is so damn bleak. Everything about it. The hopelessness, the fatalism. I thought about how back home—back in "real life" I'd say, trying to convince myself there was a difference—people would sometimes feel stuck. But you're never really stuck; it's an illusion. The people in La Segua, though—they were *stuck*, in more ways than I would ever know. They were born here and would die here, never knowing that something existed outside this life.

I thought about the times I'd lain in bed in my other life and felt alone or lonely; in La Segua, I realized that was a silly lie. I came from a world and a generation where for the most part I could write my own ticket. But in La Segua I was in the darkness and it was exactly where I was supposed to be. Something had brought me here. I had come looking for something. And now I was searching in that darkness—for something I could feel but not touch.

CHAPTER 16

After one of those long nights, I woke up to the jarring sound of Juan banging on my door. If he banged any harder, his hand would have shot through the decaying plywood. The sun was barely up yet. I rolled out from under my mosquito net as he kept on banging.

"What do you want?" I said.

"You need to go water the bamboo plants," he said, clutching a bucket in one of his giant hands. In the last few days, someone planted some of the bamboo saplings out in the wetland. Juan was very proud of this, as it had earned the association of guides a blurb in the local newspaper. (The blurb in the paper, as it happens, actually gave credit to Ignacio, Juan's number two in command, a fact that surely pissed off Juan to no end.)

"Okay, I'll do it later," I told him. I explained that I was meeting with someone else that day.

Remarkably, this was the truth. During Juan's unexplained absence, which I didn't mind, I'd begun making plans with other people. In this case, I'd been talking to a man named Nixon Dixon (seriously) about plans for improving community tourism at his integrated farm. But whether or not Nixon Dixon would show up to meet me was another story.

"No!" Juan shouted, his neck veins bulging so much that I feared they would explode, spraying blood all over me and my shirtless body.

"Your job is to go do it right now!" He threw the bucket down, sending it bouncing off the concrete and into my room.

I said under my breath in English, "Oh fuck, all right." He walked away with his crooked, massive nose held so high I wondered if he could even see the ground in front of him.

I climbed up the stairs for breakfast, where Homero was already eating. One of Juan's aunts handed me a plate of food.

"Juan's back," I said with a smile.

The aunt made a punching motion with her fist.

"What's that mean?" I asked.

Homero just shook his head.

"He wants to fight you," she said.

"For doing what?"

"He's mad at you."

"Yes," I said, "I realized. What am I supposed to do, go water the bamboo? And then what?"

The aunt didn't answer me.

Homero sat still, shaking his head and said, "What a crock of shit."

After breakfast, I carried the bucket out to the wetland, filled it up where the fishing canoes were tied, and watered the few bamboo saplings. When I came back nearly an hour later, Juan met me at the end of the driveway. "You didn't do it for long enough—go do it again."

"Look," I said, dropping the bucket at my side, "is there something you're upset about that you want to tell me?"

"We can't talk about it now," he said. "We'll talk about it later."

"No, let's talk about it now, before you disappear for a week again without telling me."

"Fine," he said, raising his voice. "Ever since you got here you haven't wanted to work with us."

"That's not true," I said. "I've done everything you've asked me to."

"But every time we go somewhere—for a meeting, to see people— you're looking for the first opportunity to leave, like you don't want to do any of the things we're doing."

"If you ever told me about these meetings in advance, then I'd be prepared for them and actually have something to contribute, instead of being there and not being involved."

"This is tourism!" he said. "We can't plan everything."

"They're meetings. If you know about them ahead of time, you could just let me know." What I'd really wanted to say was, "And where are all your tourists?"

"No. You don't need to know anything else."

"Okay," I said. "If you no longer want to work with me, that's fine. I can just continue with the obligations that I have to this community."

"You don't have any obligations to this community!" he screeched. "It was my organization"—he splayed his giant hand and thumped it across his chest—"my organization that requested you from the Peace Corps and now your only job here is to do what I tell you to do."

"Juan, you and I both know that's not true. I'm supposed to work with you and this community on several projects. I'm a volunteer, not your employee." This last line, in fact, was something the Peace Corps had specifically told us volunteers to say in the event that a conversation like this took place.

"Do you want me to call up the Peace Corps and tell them how bad you're being? Huh?" he said. "I can tell them that Grigsby Crawford isn't doing a thing he's being told to do and that he's being very bad."

I imagined for a split second how that conversation would play out and figured it would be amusing, but no one would come out looking good.

"No," I said. "I'll call my boss today and we can talk about how to work this out."

"No, no, no," Juan shouted, looking flabbergasted. "We don't need to do that."

That was all the confirmation I needed.

I went inside and took a couple of deep breaths before calling Winkler. I began by telling him that my counterpart and I were having some disagreements. I relayed the entire events of the morning to him. I told him that I'd been communicating pretty well in my time in La Segua, but that workwise, I was confronting some maturity issues with Juan, who in addition to having an interesting idea of my duty there, allegedly wanted to fight me. Somewhere during the conversation I pointed out that it was all a bit stressful.

"Yes, yes, okay, the first thing I'll just make sure is, do you feel safe in your site?" said Winkler.

I mentioned some of the vague intimidation tactics like the multiple thrown buckets. "But overall," I said, "I don't feel really threatened, no."

"Good, good," he said. "We don't need any Rambos out there."

"The awkwardness," I added, "is made a little worse with Juan living in the same house."

"What? He's still living there?" said Winkler. "All right, I'll give Juan a call this afternoon and see if we can clear all this up."

I was too caught up in the spat with Juan to realize this might have been a good time to mention the armed robberies in the neighborhood. The other thing on my mind lately was the somewhat threatening response I'd gotten when I told one of the aunts that it was customary for volunteers to leave their host families after a few months and find their own place to live. "Of course you know if you do that," she said, "you won't be with this family anymore. You might be living on the property of a family that doesn't have as much respect around here as we do. And, well, who knows what could happen to you. Bad things . . ."

I paced around the property all day, avoiding Juan and fighting the giant lump of anger and frustration that had risen in my throat. In the late afternoon when the worst heat of the day was passing, a few of the other guides came over and we used machetes to clear a field where we were supposedly going to camp out later with a group of ecotourism students.

I was bent over scraping away at the ground when Juan's phone rang; I could tell it was Winkler calling him. He went to the other end of the field to talk. I watched him. He listened. He nodded. He spoke. He used his obscene hands in gestures as if he were speaking in person. By the end, I saw him smiling and laughing. I overheard him saying how great it was to talk.

Soon after, Winkler called me back to recap his conversation with Juan. It sounded like there'd been a lot of misunderstandings, he said. It sounded like Juan was unclear on some things, but now that was all sorted out, he said. "I remain impressed—very impressed—with Juan as a counterpart," he said. My heart sank.

"So I think he's going to talk with you tonight and find a way that you guys can start from square one again and get a good working relationship going. I want to salvage this relationship because Juan is a really great counterpart." He added something else about how we had an opportunity to do important things at this site.

Before signing off, he launched into a speech unrelated to the day's incident. He talked about why he'd sent a volunteer to this site and what a fantastic resource the wetland was for these communities. It was nearly a repeat of the sales pitch he'd given me during training, after I had received my site assignment. "Oh yes," he added, "and Juan will be moving back into his parents' home. That was the agreement."

That night Juan did indeed apologize. He offered to cook me dinner but I wasn't hungry. We agreed we'd try to start over on a good foot. He hugged me. It was uncomfortable.

CHAPTER 17

That weekend, we hosted a group of students from a nearby university for the campout on the wetland. It was the first time I saw USAID money go to work. Raúl Sanchez, our intermediary with USAID, came up from Portoviejo. I later discovered he didn't work for that organization directly, but for another group it contracted out to, which had secured an entire bundle of U.S. funds to disperse among projects across the Ecuadorian coast. He used some of the funds to buy the food for the two-day/one-night campout and delivered a truckload of tents and equipment stamped with "USAID: Aid from the American People."

The few dozen students who arrived all majored in tourism at their university. The day they showed up, Juan took a couple of them out on a canoe ride, as he'd done with me on my site visit. Toward the end of the day, he made everyone gather around in a circle while he read off a list of rules. He started by reiterating that as the president of the Association of Guides of Humedal La Segua, he would be making all the final decisions that weekend. His reading of the rules lasted well over half an hour—an impressive ratio of rules-to-camping time, considering the students would be there less than twenty-four hours. With everyone fighting heat exhaustion, we finally took turns introducing ourselves.

As the budding ecotourism devotees listed off their credentials,

I began to feel enormously sad. Here we were in a country where tourism, for the most part, began and ended with a cluster of islands 1,000 kilometers off its coastline, yet someone along the way had thoroughly convinced them just the same that this was the answer. Not only that, but ecotourism (everywhere, not just in Ecuador) was becoming one of those overused phrases that no one knows the actual meaning of, like "all natural" or "clean coal."

I looked around at all this—the students, the wetland suffering from drought, overfishing and deforestation, the USAID tents. Could turning this swamp into a tourist haven ultimately help this community in the long run? Probably. But in a world where people are literally starving to death, I didn't see the virtue in tens of thousands of U.S. taxpayer dollars going toward bird watching in one of the most depraved corners of that small country.

That night I helped build a giant campfire and inevitably someone handed me a guitar and demanded that I play "Hotel California." It was about the twentieth time this had happened to me since arriving in Ecuador. Before I had a guitar, people would just ask me to sing it. Now, every time a group of people got together and a guitar was anywhere in sight, they would badger me into playing "Hotel California," just like the asshole at every concert who insists on yelling "Free Bird."

The night ended with Juan spiking an Ecuadorian flag into the ground and leading a chant about ecotourism. We all went to sleep, and the next morning we packed up the stuff and the students took off.

Back at the farm, Juan's aunts and uncles called me a faggot because I slept in a camping tent with other men. I explained that all twenty guys there, including their nephew Juan, slept in male-only tents. They only laughed more and called me a faggot again.

For nearly a month, the tension I'd been feeling caused me to clench my jaw, making it sore day and night. I had a bad feeling all over my body. And try as I did, I couldn't shake a thick, putrid, overwhelming sense of doom.

CHAPTER 18

After the campout, I sulked for a while. It was the third week of June. During those days, one of the aunts living in the house (the mother of Sandra and the pregnant teenager) mentioned that a white truck was frequently stopping in front of the property and looking around. As soon as someone spotted it, she said, the truck would speed off down the highway.

We all agreed this was suspicious. The only white truck I'd ever come across in my time there was when I was walking along the road one evening and it slowed down and swerved over next to me. A drunk guy hung out the window and said, "Hey, you motherfucking gringo. What do you want, huh? Cocaine? Marijuana? Huh, motherfucker?" I said nothing. The truck sped off as the idiot riding shotgun launched empty beer bottles at me.

When the aunt told me that we were "being watched," I asked her if there was anything we should do about it.

"No," she said. "Nothing will happen to this house. Plus, Homero has a gun and he's kind of like the family vigilante."

"Good. So he's here to protect us?"

"That's right," she said.

Returning to my room that night, I saw that yet again someone had tried breaking in. This had been going on for three straight weeks.

I could tell because I knew the number I'd left my combination lock on, and every time I got back, it was different.

The following Sunday, Homero left town for the night. That day, there'd been a local election, which, like all Ecuadorian elections, required mandatory voting. I spent another weekend doing nothing but reading in a hammock by Homero's house. On Monday night, I lay under my mosquito net listening to music.

At about ten o'clock, I got a text message from Juan. This was strange since he was upstairs, only about forty feet away.

"Grigsby, turn off your light and go to sleep," read the text. "It's very important that you stay quiet and don't leave your room. We'll talk in the morning."

Getting texts from Juan creeped me out enough as it was; one telling me to turn off my lights and go to sleep made me want to punch him in the face. So I walked upstairs to figure out what he was talking about.

"There have been some intruders on our property," he said. "And I believe they're coming for you."

"What the hell is going on?"

One of the nine people sleeping in the two rooms above me first heard footsteps behind the house while I'd been listening to music. They said they looked out the window and saw at least a couple of guys in black ski masks, carrying weapons and tiptoeing around and whispering. Once they were spotted, one ran off to the bushes, and another ran to the road, where he got into the same white pickup truck and sped away.

The family upstairs had called the Chone police. They were all huddled in the same room on the second floor. Since the teenage girls and mothers were crying hysterically, I decided it wasn't the best time to mock their comments about how no one would ever mess with the Mendoza family on their property. They were concerned about the intruder who was still lurking around somewhere nearby.

Juan and I grabbed flashlights (leftover from the campout,

compliments of USAID) onto the roof and shined them around the property down below to see if we could spot anyone. We heard rustling in the bushes every once in a while, but nothing more. After shining the flashlights for what seemed like an hour, we figured the intruders had been scared off.

But I still felt uneasy. My distrust of everyone—which had grown more in the preceding days—came pouring out as I turned to Juan. I told him, "You know I think I'm going to have to call Pilar in the morning and tell her about this."

"Are you sure?" said Juan. "Can't we just wait for the police to come and explain it to them?"

"Right, what I'm saying is that if the police get involved, I *have* to tell her."

"Okay," he said, looking skittish.

"Juan, is there anything else I should know?"

"Like what?"

"Well, do you have any idea who it might be?"

"I don't know. But I'm almost sure they were coming for you."

"If you have no idea who they were, how are you sure they were 'coming for me'?" I was so furious I could barely get out any words in Spanish.

He sighed. "There's been a lot of talk around town lately about who the gringo is and where he lives—things like that, and, well, some other things, too," he said. "They think you have a lot of money and nice things they want, so they're coming for you."

"Okay, I will definitely have to tell Pilar about this."

Before becoming Peace Corps Ecuador's head of Safety and Security, Pilar spent two decades working in antinarcotics for the national police force, where she became the highest-ranking woman. During our training, she presented several sessions on safety, covering everything from avoiding pickpockets to bus hijackings. She was kind, but I got the impression she meant business. She wore tight clothes and was sexy in a James Bond–villain type of way. I asked her once if she kept a gun in her house. She looked at me like I was an idiot and said, "Of course." Then I asked her if she'd ever used it, and I got the same look. "Grigsby, I worked in antinarcotics for twenty years." On my last day of training, I half jokingly asked her if she'd ever killed anyone with her bare hands. She just smiled.

Juan was staring at me as I pulled out my phone. "You think this might be serious?" he said.

"Yes, I have to tell her. Now, do you have any idea who the people might be?"

"No, I didn't see them."

"I'm not asking if you saw them. I'm asking if you have any *idea* who it could be. Make a guess."

"I think they could be from La Margarita," he said, referring to the neighboring town. It looked and felt like La Segua in every way, but got blamed for anything bad that happened in the area.

"Ah. They could be the same guys who raped the girl on the side of the road?"

"Yes, maybe."

"Or the guys who were robbing the houses at gunpoint?"

"Yeah, maybe." He wouldn't look me in the eye. He was staring out into the black night like the answers to my annoying questions were hidden somewhere in the trees.

"Anyone else you can think of? Any other ideas?"

Juan took a deep breath. "There are some people in this town you can't trust," he said.

No shit, I thought.

"And one of those people is Carlos," he added, referring to the neighbor and fellow ecotourism guide in my counterpart agency who rocked the rat tail/mullet. "Sometimes he does bad things," Juan continued. "He has bad friends, and, well, he's in gangs."

"What kinds of stuff do the gangs do?" I asked. I felt like wringing Juan's neck. He was clearly hiding something.

"They put on masks and stop buses in the road, then rob everyone on board at gunpoint," he said. This was such a common occurrence in Ecuador that during training, we got an entire talk about bus safety and were discouraged, among other things, from taking buses at night to avoid these holdups. "They also do other bad things," he said.

"What other kinds of bad things?"

"A while back, Carlos said we should kidnap you and see how much money we can get for you. He said it would be a good idea."

He stopped.

I waited for him to go on.

"He'd been asking us over and over again how come you hadn't given us a bunch of money yet, and I told him that that wasn't what you were here for and he said we should just go ahead and kidnap you one of these days."

"He said it just once?"

"Well, after that he kept repeating it. He kept saying he was going to do it soon, that he was going to go ahead and kidnap the gringo—you."

"He repeated this numerous times—that he wanted to kidnap me for money—in front of other people? Not just you?"

"Yes," said Juan. "A bunch of times. He was saying, 'Let's kidnap the gringo.'"

"Anything else I should know? What about these friends of his?"

"I think they were planning something like this because he was starting to sound serious."

"Why didn't you tell me about this sooner? We work with him every day."

Juan paused, then stuttered something I didn't make out. In the dim light coming from the house, I could see the veins in his neck pulsating rapidly.

I recalled a conversation I'd had a day or two earlier with none other than Carlos, who'd said to me, "You can't trust people in this area—they say one thing and do another."

"All right," I told Juan. "I'm going to call Pilar right now." It was past midnight and the Chone police still hadn't shown up. The rest of the family remained cowering in one bedroom upstairs, refusing to leave. We still couldn't tell what was lurking out there in the bushes and fields surrounding the house.

PILAR ANSWERED AFTER ONE RING and sounded unusually alert for that time of night. I apologized for calling so late and she said it wasn't a problem. We spoke in Spanish so nothing got lost in translation. I relayed everything to her, including that the cops still hadn't arrived. She proceeded to put me on hold and call the Chone police herself. (They would arrive ten minutes later apologizing for the delay.) Pilar said we'd be in touch more in a bit.

Juan and I went down to the end of the driveway to meet the police. They showed up in two pickup trucks. The blinking blue and white lights from the trucks illuminated Juan's face; he looked pale, sweaty, and frightened.

One cop did all the talking. He wore a bulletproof vest on top of a white tank top and carried a loaded machine gun.

"What happened here?" he said.

I told him. Then I asked what our next move should be.

The cop paused. "How many guns do you have around here?"

Juan chirped up to say that his uncle across the road had a gun on his property.

"Just *one* gun?" said the cop.

Juan nodded.

"Does it have bullets?"

Juan said yes. He was blinking his eyes faster than usual.

"You should have more guns on your property to protect yourself," the cop said. As he spoke he was waving his machine gun around nonchalantly. I kept backing out of the way of the barrel, so most of the conversation took place with me ducking about, trying to avoid an accidental discharge.

"Sure," I said. "More guns. Got it."

On our way back to the house, I asked Juan if he thought shots would be fired the next time someone came on the property. "We'll see," he said.

We walked the property one last time to see if anything was out of the ordinary. With mud on my boot, I slipped down the staircase of Homero's farmhouse. So much blood streamed down my arm, I felt dizzy; I held it away from my body so it wouldn't run all over me. Juan saw the blood and looked like he was going to vomit. I headed back to our house, washed it off, and then closed up the gash with a butterfly Band-Aid from my medical kit. I told Juan goodnight and went into my room.

It was the first time in my life I slept with a machete next to my bed. I kind of wished it were a gun.

CHAPTER 19

The next morning I got a call from Winkler in Quito wanting to know what the hell had happened. As I explained it, in the background I could hear him fidgeting with things on his desk.

"Do you feel safe at your site?" he said.

"No, not really," I told him. "It'd be one thing if this were some idiot or the town drunk making kidnapping threats, but this is a guy I'm supposed to work with. So no, I don't feel very safe right now, unfortunately."

"Hmm. Okay," he said.

A couple of hours later, I received a text message from the country director: "Pilar will be at your site tomorrow to investigate. If you see that white truck again, call us immediately." The prospect of Pilar coming out to "investigate" thrilled me. My heart raced.

The following morning Homero got back home from his brief trip down the coast. One of the other family members filled him in on the previous night's events. In the evening, he and I stood in the driveway and talked.

"I heard everyone was freaking out last night, like *please don't kill me*," he said, waving his hands about. "What a bunch of pussies you all are. Pussies!"

"I wouldn't say I was *freaking out*. But since your whole family was upstairs crying, someone had to take responsibility around here."

"No one's going to do anything to this family on this property."

"So I've heard. But why, then, were they wearing masks and carrying weapons?"

"Eh, it's all a bunch of bullshit."

"All right, well, just make sure you have your gun ready tonight," I said. "We've got some machetes in the main house but I don't think they'll do the trick."

"Listen, Crawford, if someone wanted to kill you they would have already done it. So don't—"

"That's nice—"

"Look, just think about how easy it would be," Homero said. "All they'd have to do is reach inside your window there"—he pointed to my first-floor bedroom a few yards away—"while you're sleeping and BOOM!" He formed a gun with his hand and reached to fake-fire a bullet into my skull.

"So don't worry! Like I said, someone would have already killed you if they wanted. Easy! For instance"—and here my ears perked up, because when the topic is murder and someone says "for instance," what follows is bound to be a treat—"some time ago when a guy had a problem with the person who lived over there"—Homero pointed to the farmhouse next to our property—"he just walked in one night and shot him in the face." He snapped his fingers. "It was that easy."

"Thanks for the advice."

I slept poorly that night and got up early the next day. In an astonishing display of tact, that was the first and only morning Esteban didn't tell me he killed gringos for fun. All day I waited for Pilar to come blazing into town in one of the Peace Corps' silver Toyota 4-Runners. When she did, a man was riding shotgun; Pilar introduced him as "the Colonel." He was an old associate of hers in the national police who had trained at Quantico, Virginia, and was now head of a private security firm based out of Manta (a port town not far from us that was an infamous drug trafficking jump-off point).

When I met up with the security duo, I was in San Antonio, a small town between La Segua and Chone. Pilar had instructed me to meet them on a street corner, where she found me and told me to get in the back of the car. I went over the story of Juan, Carlos, and the intruders again as she cruised through a neighborhood at about five miles an hour; she didn't want to stop and be spotted or trailed. While I spoke, she and the Colonel looked at me in the rear-view mirror.

I discovered that by the time they'd picked me up, Pilar had already been to La Segua and interviewed most of my host family and neighbors about the situation. After asking me a few questions, she picked up Juan and interrogated him while he sat next to me in the back. Juan stumbled over his words a lot. The Colonel blew plumes of cigarette smoke out the window and glared at Juan through the visor mirror.

Pilar had one more interview to do after finishing with Juan and me. She drove us back to the house in La Segua, dropped us off, and continued down the road to talk to Carlos.

Pilar returned around dusk. We stood out in the chicken shit–covered driveway. Dust kicked up and the sun began to set.

"It's not safe for you here," she said. "These people . . ." Her voice trailed off and she shook her head. We both took in panoramic views of the decrepit scenery. We were standing in the same spot where Homero and I had talked the day before.

Thinking about that conversation, I said, "Yeah, it also makes me a little worried that my room is on the bottom floor here and someone could easily just reach through the window and—"

"You're living on the bottom floor?" she said. "Oh no, no, no."

Pilar explained that she had approved another room for me when she did a security check before I arrived. Normally, which room of the house I slept in would be trivial. But in this case it made all the difference. The room on the second floor, which was currently occupied by about nine Mendozas, was where she'd told Juan I had to live. It had its own bathroom and a real door. She'd wanted me up there, not in the dungeon room on the bottom floor, for exactly the reason Homero had illustrated in the driveway a day earlier. The only reason I'd never said anything about the room was because it's what I'd expected out of the Peace Corps. I didn't want to sound like a wimp. (When I later showed pictures of my bedroom and bathroom to another volunteer, she said she would have Early Terminated after one day.)

Pilar called Juan out of the house to have a word with him. She asked him why he'd had me move into that room on the bottom floor.

"Uh, I know what you said, but we didn't know exactly when he was coming and—"

"Stop talking," said Pilar. "You've been lying to him this whole time about which room he was supposed to be living in?"

I echoed the sentiment: "On my site visit, you told me it was the room Pilar had approved . . ."

I saw true fear in Juan's eyes and the wheels turning in his head. It was slowly dawning on him that he could lose the gringo he'd been toting around like a prized possession all this time.

Juan mumbled a little more and Pilar walked all over him verbally. It was fun to watch. She told Juan to go away and pulled me aside to say she'd talk to the country director that night. Pilar was going to tell her that it wasn't safe for me here, and in the morning, they'd make a final decision on whether to pull me out.

Pilar and the Colonel drove off as the sun went down over the wetland. I walked back into the house where, to my surprise, my whole host family of aunts and teen mothers began screaming at me.

"By making the cops come here, you've ruined our reputation," they cried. "Now everyone will assume we're involved in criminal activity." They grew hysterical.

Particularly upset was Evelyn, the pregnant fifteen-year-old whose belly was ready to burst any day now. "Why the hell did you tell the police about the father of my child? That lady comes in here saying stuff like, 'I hear your baby's father was into some drugs and crime. Is it possible he's jealous and could be causing trouble for you?' What's that bullshit all about? Huh?"

"First of all, Pilar works for the Peace Corps, not the police. Second, no, I didn't tell her anything about your boyfriend."

"He's not my boyfriend."

"Oh, right, he's dead."

"Well if you didn't tell her, then who did?" she said.

The answer seemed pretty obvious. Juan, who'd frantically told Pilar just about every detail of every person living in the house over the phone the night before, sat there silently while all this went on. I looked at him, waiting for him to say something. He didn't.

"Look, I don't know what to tell you," I said. "Pilar was just doing her job." Evelyn was yelling so loudly now that she began to lisp. Then more aunts entered the room and joined in, firing words at me. I couldn't understand what anybody was saying.

Finally Juan piped up. "This is all going to be okay." No one listened.

I went downstairs and locked myself in my room for the rest of the night. I could still hear the yelling through the floorboards.

In the morning, Winkler called again to check in.

I was sick of talking at this point, but I told him everything that had gone down the day before with Pilar.

"How do you feel there?" he said.

"Not good. Everybody's freaking out. I should get out of here to somewhere I can actually be an effective volunteer. No one should have been here in the first place."

"But this is normal," he said.

I was stunned. He was still trying to get me to stay in La Segua—like he wanted to prove that his idea to send me there wasn't a failure.

"These types of misunderstandings are common," he said. "This stuff happens all the time with new sites." He added some stuff about being able to salvage the situation.

"I don't think this is normal," I said. "Pilar has confirmed that much, I know."

"Have you tried talking it out with this guy Carlos?" he said. "Are you going to let just one incident spoil your whole working relationship with the counterpart agency? We can't just give up on this site and this counterpart organization like this!"

"Talk it out? I—well, Pilar told me to avoid anything like that for now. She told me to leave all that up to her."

Winkler ended the conversation by grumbling something about how site changes were, ideally, a last resort and how he wanted to do everything possible to keep me in La Segua, because any other outcome would be a big hassle and generally an undesirable situation for him, as the program manager, to be in.

Soon after, the country director called. She said she'd been talking to Pilar and they were assessing the situation. Before she made her final decision on whether to pull me out of the site and find a new place, she just wanted to check in and see what I had to say. I told her about the day before with Pilar and what had happened after she left.

"My goodness, they were yelling and screaming at you?" She added something else about having spoken with Winkler as well.

"Something else I think I should add," I said, "is that I don't think Winkler and I are really seeing eye to eye on the whole situation. He seems to think that this is one big misunderstanding."

She said okay, then asked a few more questions she already knew the answers to. We ended our conversation and an hour later she called back.

"Pack up all your belongings," she said. "Pilar will be there soon to pick you up."

In the early afternoon, Pilar cruised down the dusty driveway once again, this time without the Colonel. She wore tight black capris, high heels, and Ray Bans. She took off the sunglasses and said, "*Vamos.*"

I said goodbye to the host family. After screaming at me the night before, they seemed sad and nostalgic to see me go. Perhaps it was the forty dollars of monthly rent they'd be missing out on. (This, by the way, was another one of Juan's lies that irked Pilar. They'd agreed on thirty-five dollars during Pilar's initial visit, but Juan upped the sum without her permission when I showed up.)

"Will you visit us?" asked the aunts.

"Yes," I lied.

Juan wasn't at home that day, so Pilar called him on her cell phone as we drove east toward Chone. She told Juan the Peace Corps had made the decision to remove the volunteer due to safety concerns.

She added that it didn't help that he'd spent so much of his time lying. When he grows up and is ready, she told him, the Peace Corps may still be available to his organization. Juan argued about something; I couldn't quite overhear. Pilar talked over him and shook her head. Her closing line was the single greatest sentence I've ever heard spoken in Spanish: "The safety and security of my volunteers is *numero uno.*"

While Pilar drove she said to me, "This is the right decision. The country director and I agree. But Winkler, he's not very happy about this, I don't think."

"Really?"

"Winkler," she said, shaking her head. "He just doesn't get it."

Pilar had to leave the Peace Corps vehicle in Guayaquil where she would take a flight back to Quito, so she dropped me at the Chone bus station and I caught the next ride to Quito.

Two and a half hours outside Chone, the bus driver pulled into a roadside diner and told everyone to grab their luggage because there was something wrong with the bus and he needed to go down the road to fix it. After an hour of waiting, we passengers figured out the bus wasn't coming back. Police arrived. One woman began screaming at the police about how "this government promised us that citizens would have *rights!*"

A few others and I hitched a ride into Santo Domingo where we caught a different bus headed for Quito. A car accident along the way turned what is normally a seven-hour bus ride into a ten-hour one. I got to Quito at 2 a.m. and checked into a hotel a few blocks from the Peace Corps headquarters. I spent the next ten days sitting in the office and wandering around Quito waiting for Winkler, in all his wisdom, to find me a new site.

I'd lived in La Segua for less than eight weeks. At the time, I didn't know what to make of what had happened there, but before long everything about the place would come back to haunt me.

PART TWO

The Pain

CHAPTER 20

I traveled down the spine of the Andes for twelve hours before turning east and descending into the Amazon for another few hours. The province of Zamora Chinchipe is Ecuador's most isolated—hidden away in the southeast corner of the country against the Peruvian border. The bus followed the Pan American Highway south until it reached Loja, the country's southernmost city of any significance. From there, I boarded a different bus and rode for three and a half hours, passing through several in-progress landslides on the way to Zamora, the provincial capital, and then another hour northeastward to my new site, Zumbi. This was my first time in the Ecuadorian Amazon, and it looked exactly the way I thought the South American jungle should.

Not knowing the town, I'd been asking other passengers if we were there yet for the forty-five minutes preceding our arrival. To enter Zumbi, you turn right off the highway (essentially the only main road that runs through the province) and cross a bridge that goes over the Rio Zamora, which snakes down through the mountains all the way from Loja. On the other side of the bridge is a town square with a church at the far end. Buses go around the square and stop on the side where the street vendors (and their litter) sit.

I arrived late in the morning. The sky was overcast and the air was cool with a light drizzle. I would later find out that these were the best mornings of all because the alternatives were either heat so penetrating that I'd stick to my sheets or rain so violent I had no choice but to avoid the outdoors altogether. The four-block-by-four-block town of Zumbi sits along the river, nestled between tall lush mountains on all sides. On days like this, wispy clouds hang low above the valley with the green mountaintops exposed on top.

My host family lived three blocks off the main square and in those three blocks, the sound of car horns and blaring reggaeton music disappeared and the roads turned from stone to dirt. Zumbi went from a miniature city to something resembling the rustic countryside, or *campo*, you'd expect from a Peace Corps site. A few of the houses were made of wood and corrugated tin, but most were one-story concrete blocks. Extending above from the first and only floor would be concrete pillars and exposed rebar that could potentially be the beginnings of a second level. It was as though they'd left that area unfinished in hopes that one day they would have the resources to fill it in. But based on the age of the homes and the rust dripping from the rebar, the second stories rarely became a reality.

I would be living with a grandmother named Graciela and her thirty-five-year-old daughter, Consuela, who was a local politician and a mother of three. Recently widowed, Graciela spent her free time walking through town wearing a giant red-and-white antiabortion shirt with the Pope's face on one side and a child's on the other. As I would come to find out, Graciela and Consuela did not exactly get along. In fact, they hated each other.

The family had two dogs at the house: Jack and Benji. Both were eerie mixes of opposing breeds that should never have been let near each other, creating ugly little animals that seemed to know that they'd been dealt a terrible hand in life. Jack was a big, mean-looking animal and Benji was small and gentle. Consuela once told me that Benji was either gay or "just metrosexual."

That first day, I entered the front gate and Graciela showed me to my room on the second floor. It was the Ritz-Carlton compared to what I had in La Segua. Painted walls instead of exposed brick. Linoleum floors instead of concrete. A bathroom that would occasionally have sewage backups—but it was better than my old outhouse. Windows I could look through and see the jungle hills.

Like almost every family in the town, I would come to find out, this one had relatives that either had lived or were currently living in Spain. From there, they would send home sums of money, and then several years later, they'd come home for good and use their savings to splurge on their properties in Zumbi. Consuela had lived for some time in Spain (where her third child was born), and three of her brothers currently lived there (one of them, I later discovered, would be there indefinitely because he was a fugitive in Ecuador). Thus, their house was one of the "nicer" ones in town. However, this usually just meant that they'd used their saved-up Euros to put a new façade on the same house they'd always had. Look around the side of the house and you'd see the same cinder-block walls that covered every other building in the area.

I WOKE UP AFTER MY first night in Zumbi and met up with two volunteers who lived in Zamora Chinchipe for an up-river excursion. We rode a truck two hours east to the site of the next closest volunteer in the province. From there, we drove another hour to where the road ended and got in a motorized canoe and rode for a couple of hours before getting out to hike near the Peruvian border. At one point our guide said not to go off the trail because of land mines; this was the lingering result of a nearly century-old border dispute between the two countries.

The hike was a pleasant first look at the Amazon. We saw snakes. We saw waterfalls. We saw an indigenous community where my fellow volunteer had previously witnessed a failed suicide attempt. We almost ran out of gas. It rained. I got back to my site late at night.

I opened the front gate to the property of my house and walked across the yard to reach the outside stairs leading up to my room. Before I could make it, I was cut off by a flying dog. Jack—the big, mean one—had gotten a running start from about ten feet away. His open jaws went straight for my left arm, and he landed a slobbery bite on my triceps. The only move I could make at the time to defend myself was several kicks in Jack's direction. I probably landed a half-dozen good blows before Consuela came racing across the yard screaming and nearly crying. She began lashing Jack with the type of whip you see lion tamers use at circuses.

Consuela frantically asked me if I was okay. I said I was; Jack's bite hadn't broken the skin. She grabbed him by the neck and took him over to the wash area and tied him to a post. Benji, meanwhile, cowered at the far end of the front yard. Consuela kept apologizing as she tied up the dog. I repeated that I was fine and walked to my room.

Graciela and Consuela took off the following day and didn't say when they were coming back. They left Jack chained to the post near the washbasin and didn't give me any directions for feeding him. I woke up the next day to the sound of Jack's whimpers as Benji pranced around the property looking for attention.

With time, the whimpers became more intense and I began to feel bad for Jack. I also felt bad about the several roundhouses to the muzzle I'd landed during his attack on me. But I didn't feel safe enough letting him loose. I finally went out and gave him some food and some TLC. After a few days of this, he was my friend.

The first night Graciela and Consuela were gone, I awoke to the sound of a madman at our front gate. He was screaming for Consuela and rattling the fence and throwing rocks at our house. I peered down at him through my bedroom window. All I could think was, *Oh shit, not again.* But after a midnight call to Consuela to find out what the fuck was going on (and a visit from some trusted neighbors), I found out that he was merely a man with "many demons" (Consuela's words) who often "became confused" and came calling for her in the night.

When the two women returned, Consuela apologized profusely for the madman's midnight visit. And both she and her mother were amazed at the transformation I'd made in Jack.

CHAPTER 21

The Peace Corps sent me to Zumbi to work for a government project called the Fund for Child Development, referred to by its Spanish acronym FODI. Essentially, it was a government-run rural childcare service. Their main office was in the municipal building, and in smaller communities throughout the countryside, they directed a dozen centers where parents dropped off their toddlers in the morning and picked them up in the afternoon after work. At a FODI center, the children were bathed and fed. They also played educational games and learned basic things like the alphabet.

On my first day, I went to the office and met everyone in FODI. The municipality took up a four-story yellow building on the outskirts of town. Surrounded as it was by jungle foothills, dirt roads, and the crumbling wood and cinder-block buildings in the rest of Zumbi, the structure looked strikingly out of place.

The FODI office was filled with women. The project leader, Jenny, was in her late thirties, and the six other women were all about that age or younger. I introduced myself and they stared back at me. In Quito, Winkler's assistant had told me to be careful with the women there because they were very flirty, and when he'd visited the site months before, they were calling him things like "stud muffin" minutes after meeting him.

I went around the room trying to remember names. They asked

me mine; I told them and they proceeded to call me . . . stud muffin.
They wanted to know about Kathy, another volunteer who'd gone to
Zumbi for her site visit but had gotten kicked out of the Peace Corps
the night before we swore in. Kathy's dismissal was the only reason
Zumbi was available as an approved site for me after the La Segua
calamity. Back in training, the Peace Corps was unhappy that Kathy
had ditched Spanish class one morning and gotten caught drinking
beer in Cayambe. After this incident, the training manager went to
her host family and found her bedroom too messy, to the extent that
it was deemed culturally insensitive (seriously), and thus grounds for
Administrative Separation. Understandably, the women in FODI were
confused about having Kathy visit for three days back in March only
to never return and then four months later getting a man in her place.

I told the women I thought Kathy had had some medical issues
that forced her to go home. Winkler suggested that I have an answer
like this handy when they asked me about it.

"I couldn't figure out why the Peace Corps had sent me a woman
in the first place," Jenny said. "I asked for a male volunteer."

"You requested a man?" I said.

"Yes," she said.

At home I dug back into my files, including the volunteer solicita-
tion that I'd never looked at very closely. Indeed, FODI had made only
one request: a male volunteer. They didn't list a single other tangible
skill or attribute that they needed the volunteer to have. They didn't
even care whether the volunteer came from the sustainable agriculture program or the natural resource conservation program—as long
as he was male.

After introducing myself the first day, I stood in the middle of
the room and asked what they wanted me to do. They all smiled and
looked at me. No one answered until Jenny hemmed and hawed and
told me to come back tomorrow (I would get told to "come back tomorrow" almost every other day at FODI).

The next day we drove two hours east into the hills to a community named San Francisco. Of all the towns in the county, this one was

farthest from Zumbi. It had no more than a hundred people, mostly indigenous. A couple of the women from the FODI office jotted down notes after talking to the teachers who worked full time in the center. The teachers cooked us lunch. My plate had a mysterious meat on it, and when I asked my FODI colleagues what it was, they laughed. I asked again and they laughed even harder. This went on for several minutes until a woman next to me whispered that it was cow intestine. Someone across the table reached over and ate it off my plate.

Before we left, a deaf woman came to the center and got in an argument with one of the FODI workers. They were going back and forth with dramatic hand signals that definitely weren't formal sign language. Apparently, the woman wanted to know why her child wasn't allowed to go to the FODI center, and the worker was trying to convey to her that it was because the child was over five years old. The grunts and violent hand gestures went on for a few more minutes and we got back in the truck and drove home to Zumbi.

AFTER A WEEK OF BEING driven out into the countryside with the FODI workers and not doing anything, I got in touch with a volunteer who lived in my province and had worked with this FODI office in the past. I asked her if she had any idea what they wanted me to do for them—it was the same thing I'd asked Jenny and the other workers a number of times and only gotten giggles in response.

"Well, they just wanted some male energy in the office," she said.

"*Male energy?*"

"Uh-huh."

"They just wanted a guy around to flirt with?"

"Pretty much, yeah," she said.

"What did you do for them?"

"I used to give some lessons on nutrition to the mothers of the FODI kids," she said. "Then I started bringing a book of crossword puzzles with me when we traveled out to the centers."

"And they didn't ask anything else of you?"

"The thing is, for them, it's good that we're even around. We are basically doing a job by just being here—you know, goals two and three."

She was referring to the three goals of the Peace Corps that had existed unchanged since its legendary JFK-era inception. The first goal is the one that talks about alleviating poverty in poor countries. The second and third refer to sharing our culture with the host country and in turn sharing the host country's culture with Americans back home. Among volunteers I knew, it'd become a bit of an inside joke: When they weren't doing any actual projects in their communities, they said they were "working hard on goals two and three." As with most jokes, it had a message: Here's an organization that didn't know whether it was an actual development agency or an ambassadorial program where your main job was to go to some community and just *chill* (which, after all, fulfilled a whopping 66 percent of your stated objectives).

This volunteer, however, wasn't joking.

I continued to go to FODI every day of the week for about two months. I tried to start community vegetable gardens with the teachers, but it usually rained too hard. A few times I gave presentations to the mothers of the FODI children about how to make compost in their homes or about the most fundamental environmental education lesson I could think of: reduce, reuse, recycle. But mostly, I just kept hearing "come back tomorrow."

CHAPTER 22

When the days got long and the rain let up and I had nothing to do, I spent a lot of time walking around Zumbi. In case it wasn't odd enough to have a white American, out of nowhere, living in their community, the town's inhabitants were now treated to this strange creature wandering aimlessly at all hours of the day without any particular destination.

I passed them as they sat—on curbs in front of dusty streets, on splintered wooden benches in front of one-room concrete houses, in plastic chairs on the sidewalk. And they stared. At me. The gringo.

The town of Zumbi is several dozen acres cut out of the jungle, located on the western end of a 291-square-kilometer county that's 75 percent deforested. The hills surrounding Zumbi are part of the Cordillera del Condor, a range of mountains formed independently of the Andes thousands of years ago.

From my house, I could walk southward to the other far end of town. I would pass an elementary school with paint peeling off the walls and murals that announced both the glorious nature of Zumbi, the "Ecological Garden of the Amazon," and an opposition to abortion. I passed store after store, each selling the same things: milk, candy, toilet paper, Coca-Cola, and bread. I passed stray dogs that came after me barking savagely until I picked up a rock and they scattered away; I passed other dogs too hungry to lift themselves up off the sidewalk. I passed a bar that had empty bottles of several exotic liquors on the shelf, but really sold only one drink: Pilsener, Ecuador's national beer of choice.

I passed by tiny restaurants that served the same thing as the restaurant a block down from them: boiled chicken and rice. I passed row after row of crumbling cinder-block houses, interrupted only by the mayor's hulking, multistory, brand-new, Mediterranean-style mansion, which was squeezed in between an abandoned lot and a one-room wooden shack on the other side. (The mayor's annual salary was about $40,000, or nearly fifteen times the salary of the average citizen in Zumbi.)

I passed by miniature hardware stores—lots of them. For a town of around a thousand, there were nearly a dozen hardware stores all selling the exact same products, from paint to barbed-wire to gardening tools. The lack of entrepreneurial diversity is something you see a lot of in Latin America—a guy will open a hardware store simply because his friend down the street has the same business, not realizing that if they each had a unique business, both would make more money—but Zumbi's oversaturated market of hardware stores was like nothing I'd ever seen. It's a town where the water and power go out on a weekly basis and people all over the place are coming down with bizarre illnesses, but if you ever need a shovel or a screw driver, you needn't walk more than forty yards.

I passed by a chicken, or *pollo*, establishment with a sign out front that, due to a mixture of upper- and lowercase letters, appeared to say that they had "Polio for sale." I passed by a store that sold bootlegged CDs and had converted its back room into a makeshift arcade by setting up a couple of dusty XBOXes with old TV monitors and plastic chairs in front. I passed by children playing soccer, or kicking dogs, or yelling at me in broken English, "Hello, gringo!" or "Good morning, teacher," even when it was late at night (and even though I wasn't their teacher). I passed by barefoot drunken men with food smeared on their faces who yelled, "Hey, gringo, come drink, c'mon, just come drink, here have a drink." I passed by women between the ages of ten and sixty who made catcalls at me.

Four blocks past the park and away from the river, things abruptly turn from city to countryside. Since the municipal building is at the far end of town, it's surrounded by the farmland that extends from the outer edges of Zumbi up into the hills where farmers grow corn and bananas and cacao, but mostly tear down trees to make room for cattle grazing.

I walked up and down each of these blocks, sometimes saying hello to people only to have them stare blankly back at me.

And one day I walked into an old building on the edge of town that had history books and old newspaper clips about the region (along with a surprisingly large amount of Scientology material). I peeled back the dusty pages and read about the land and the people, going back hundreds of years to when the first inhabitants spilled over the Andes and into this part of the Amazon.

Those first people were the Shuar—an indigenous group best known for shrinking the heads of their enemies after battle. Later, of course, the Spanish arrived—changing the religion, language, and bloodlines in the area forever.

Then I read about the country's independence, and it explained the strange maps I'd seen hanging in classrooms, with Ecuador's southeastern border not in its usual spot but instead bulging far out into Peru's Amazon territory. This cartographic aggression resulted from over a century of border disputes between the two countries that had caused military skirmishes close to Zumbi as recently as the '90s. The disagreement was ultimately put to rest with a peace treaty in 1998. Now, more than a decade later, for one of the country's most isolated provinces, Zamora Chinchipe remains heavily militarized, with small army bases dotting the hillsides and lining the rivers in even the most obscure locales.

Zamora Chinchipe didn't really start to grow until the '80s, when modern mining got underway. But in the three decades since, its population has increased to only about 75,000, making it mainland Ecuador's second-least populated province, despite being one of the four largest in land mass.

Zumbi's county, Centinela del Condor, was the smallest in Zamora Chinchipe. Up until the '90s, Zumbi had looked the same for several decades. It began as farmland with small houses scattered here and there. Eventually more jungle was hacked away and what is now the location of the central park began to take shape. Soon the church was built and a few other wooden buildings came in around it. But the lack of a car bridge had a moat-like effect on Zumbi, preventing it and everything to its east from developing as quickly as the rest of the province. And nowadays, the only remnant of the Shuar in the area is its name—*zumbi* was the Shuar word for a type of fish that was once abundant in the Rio Zamora—and a tiny Shuar village located in the hills an hour east of Zumbi. When I'd visited the village with FODI, it was the saddest, poorest place I encountered in Ecuador—complete with food being boiled in outdoor cauldrons over burning trash and thirteen-year-old mothers without shoes.

What I didn't read about the history of the area, I learned from listening to some of the old men I passed on the streets. They were among the original settlers who'd come to build roads or mine for gold or shoot at Peruvian helicopters decades ago. And they had watched as bridges got built, roads got paved, and more people moved in.

CHAPTER 23

I was adjusting to life in Zumbi. By late August I'd spent more time (eight weeks) in my new site than I had in my coastal nightmare. I also eclipsed the half-year-in-country mark and somehow convinced myself this milestone meant something.

It didn't.

The days were long and I had less and less work with FODI. The constant rain from my first months in Zumbi gave way to a penetrating jungle heat. Shop owners would hang large plastic tarps in their storefronts to shield themselves from the blinding sun. Zumbi usually moved in slow motion, and the heat slowed it down even more. Even the buses passing through town were never in a hurry to get anywhere. They idled near the side of the road for up to forty-five minutes, filling the most crowded street in town with gasoline fumes.

Because I didn't feel entirely comfortable cooking in Graciela and Consuela's roach-infested kitchen, I would eat out at the roadside cafés frequently. It was a good way for me to meet people in the community. Plus, a full meal was dirt cheap. For just two dollars, I'd get a heaping plate of chicken and rice—with a serving of questions on the side.

"Where are you from?"

I told them.

"Ah, American."

"Yes."

"What are you doing here?"

I explained.

"Do you like it here?"

Early on, I would answer this question by playing into their intracountry xenophobia: "I was living on the coast and I had some security issues, so now I'm here and I like it much better."

"Yes," they'd say. "Bad people on the coast. Can't trust 'em. Bad, dirty, violent people. Here, the people are nice."

Then they'd lay into me with the real kickers. And it would go something like this:

"Is the United States bigger than Ecuador?"

Or: "Does the United States border an ocean?"

And then: "Have you met Arnold Schwarzenegger?"

"Actually, yes," I'd say, and they'd ignore me to jump to the next, apparently rhetorical, question.

"Which part of the U.S. are you from?"

"A state called Colorado, in the West," I'd say.

"I can't pronounce that," they'd say. "Cow-loo . . . what?"

"It's a Spanish word," I'd say. "You have a province here that used to have the same word in it—*Santo Domingo de los Colorados*."

"Oh, Colorado," they'd say. And then, "Do you have black people in the U.S.?"

One night while I was at one of the two watering holes in Zumbi, I put my beer on the table, looked at the wall, and saw a Che Guevara poster. It was taped up between ones of Christina Aguilera and MTV's Lauren Conrad. I asked the owner if she liked Che.

"Love him," she said.

"So are you a fan of Rafael Correa?" I asked. Correa, their president (and University of Illinois, Champaign-Urbana alumnus), is known as a leftist.

"No, no," she said. "I voted for—" She named one of the other half-dozen dudes who had just run unsuccessfully against Correa. The guy she named was to the right.

"You voted for the right-wing candidate?" I said.

"*Sí!*"

"But you think Che is the man?"

"*Sí!*"

ONCE, IN A RESTAURANT, I had a conversation that went like this:

Teenage girl: "Where are you from?"

Me: "The U.S."

Girl: "Ah, and do you speak English?"

Me: "Yes, it's our country's primary language." (Had I been in a more chipper mood, I might have added the surely mind-blowing statistic that the U.S. also had thirty million *more* Spanish speakers than Ecuador.)

Girl: "Cool, do you speak Spanish as well?"

Me: "Yes . . . wait, what?"

Girl: "Spanish. Do you speak it?"

Me: "We've been speaking Spanish the entire time I've been sitting here."

Girl: "So do you speak Spanish?"

Me: "I guess not."

I finished my meal in silence.

I TRIED MY BEST TO rotate between the very few eating venues in the town. Only on one occasion did my dining experience force me to boycott a location.

As I was finishing the food on my plate, the cook/waiter (he was the only other person in the restaurant at the time) came from behind the counter and sat down across from me. He had long hair and looked like an emaciated version of Carlos Santana.

"Gringo?"

"Yes."

"Girlfriend?"

"No."

"So then what do you do?" He smiled with raised eyebrows and the vaguely detached look of someone who had no idea how creepy he was.

"What do you mean?"

"What do you do to . . . you know?"

"Are you asking if I go to the whorehouses?" I said.

"Maybe."

"No, I don't."

"Oh, I see. So then what do you do?" He made an exaggerated jerking-off motion with his hand.

"You want to know if I jerk off?"

His eyes widened, like I'd just breached some taboo subject.

"It's only because I heard gringos have big ones." He motioned with his hands about a yard apart and then brought them together to suggest a girth that would make even a mare wince.

"Really?" I began pushing my chair out to stand up and leave.

"I bet you have a big one. Do you have a big cock? I bet you've got one, don't you."

I stood up.

"Have I offended you?"

"Oh no, not at all," I said, starting to walk out.

"I'm very sorry," he said, "it's just that—" He motioned again with his hands suggesting a whale-sized member.

I headed for the door. I forget whether I paid.

CHAPTER 24

At the end of August, everyone in the FODI office was fired, along with nearly all the other workers in the municipality.

A month before I arrived in Zumbi, they'd had an election and the sitting mayor—a man named Raúl—lost. I'd hung out with Raúl a bit, most notably when we were on the same team in a game of pickup basketball and he was smoking a cigarette *while playing*.

The fact that he lost struck me as odd at first since he was in the same party as President Correa, who had enormous support in the area. I later found out that Raúl had participated in numerous extramarital affairs with municipal workers over his five-year term. During his race for reelection, the opposition—a young political novice with a law degree—based his entire campaign on painting Raúl as an adulterer and well-known wife beater (when I first got to town, I was confused by the graffiti on buildings that said "Enough with Raúl and the disrespect to women," but it finally made sense when someone told me all this months afterward). The opposing candidate's scathing refrain was that Raúl had been "running the municipality like a whorehouse." Incredibly, despite all this, Raúl was nearly reelected. The difference-maker on Election Day came from the town of San Pablo, where the young candidate supposedly received four hundred votes from the hundred or so registered voters.

In any event, the new mayor came in and, per tradition, removed all municipal workers who didn't support him in the election—even the janitors. So all the FODI women were gone and I was left with no one to "work" with.

When I was in Quito, waiting on my site change, Winkler talked to me about working with FODI and warned me that this might happen. "They'll likely be replaced," he said. At that point, the election had already taken place; I arrived in Zumbi in the interim while the old mayor still had a few more months left and the new mayor had yet to swear in.

"It's just the way politics work here, unfortunately," said Winkler. He suggested that in those first few months, I use FODI to make some contacts within the municipality for work I could do down the road.

Given that conversation, I was pretty confused the first time Winkler called and asked how things were going in the office. I told him I was looking for new projects to do because of the firings. His response: "What! They've been fired? Then who . . . I mean, what are you going to . . . I mean, who exactly are you going to be working with? This just isn't good. It's no good. We've got to find you someone to be working with. And fast!"

AT HOME, THINGS BETWEEN CONSUELA and Graciela had fully deteriorated. Their screaming matches and dog abuse became more frequent and it was getting under my skin. But I couldn't move out. When I changed sites, the clock got reset on my Peace Corps–mandated three-month stay with a host family. On top of that, it would likely be an even longer wait for me to find a new place since only program managers or their assistants could approve new housing. The program managers were obligated to visit our sites within those first three months, but between my site changing and Winkler stalling on taking the trip down to my part of the country, I was approaching eight months without a visit from a program manager.

During that time, the household had grown by one: Consuela's sixteen-year-old goddaughter, Lucia. She came from San Eduardo, a tiny rural community about an hour and a half from Zumbi that I'd visited with FODI and seen more kids walking barefoot through piles of trash. Lucia had come to stay with Consuela and Graciela indefinitely while she finished her high school degree on Saturdays, meaning that six days a week, she moped around the house because Consuela and Graciela didn't want her leaving without them.

One morning while I was eating alone in the kitchen, Lucia—who mumbled and spoke so poorly she sometimes said four sentences before I figured out what she was talking about—decided she trusted me. She leaned close to me and whispered, "How do you stand it here?"

"What are you talking about?" I said.

"You know, with Graciela, Consuela, and the constant fighting," she said. "Graciela—she's so . . . mean."

A few weeks after she arrived, Lucia came to me as soon as Graciela and Consuela had left the house. She told me she couldn't take the yelling and the fighting anymore and was "running away"—presumably, back to San Eduardo where the rest of her family was from. I asked her why she didn't just tell Graciela or Consuela that she wanted to go back home, and she said they wouldn't let her. So she left a note on Graciela's bed that said she couldn't stand the way they treated her and was leaving. Consuela came home first and found the note and went ballistic. Graciela was indifferent.

The very next day, Lucia came back. Apparently, she was done running away.

Graciela had been growing increasingly bitter since about a month after I'd moved in. In that first month, because everything seemed normal, and the house—remodeled with money her kids earned in Spain—was as nice a place as I would ever find in Zumbi, I signed a rental contract with Graciela that would last through April 2011, till the end of my service. Graciela read the contract, signed it, and welcomed me into their home. She asked me what I liked to eat, and I said, don't worry, I'll cook for myself. She asked me how I'd clean my clothes, and I told her I could wash them. I'd already done the host-family scenario twice in Ecuador, so I felt more comfortable as a sort of tenant than as a gringo quasi-family member once again.

Aside from the little water and electricity I used, it was almost like they didn't have another person living with them. My room was detached from theirs, so they didn't see me if they didn't want to. I didn't have visitors because I had no friends. I wasn't noisy and even if I were, they couldn't have heard it downstairs and across a patio. When I was done eating, I washed and put away my dishes, and when they used the kitchen, I stayed out of their way and came back later.

But somewhere in there—perhaps because I didn't go to church with Graciela every Sunday or because I'd said no thank you to her cooking—she hated my guts.

After making my breakfast one morning and leaving the kitchen cleaner than I found it, Graciela ambushed me.

"I'm trying to get new people to come and live in your room," she said.

"Why?" I asked. "I thought I'd be able to stay until the date we agreed on in the contract."

She ignored the whole "contract" business and said that these new people were going to pay her $60 a month—three times more than the $20 I was paying, per the agreement Winkler made with Graciela when he came down to approve the site.

"Okay," I said, "does that mean that if I pay $60 I can stay?" Admittedly, $20 was a lowball price considering volunteers with "rural" sites like mine were allotted up to $70 a month. Whether I paid $20 or $70 made no difference to me because it was deposited into my bank account separate from my normal monthly living allowance.

"Maybe," said Graciela. She wrinkled her forehead, and the fake eyebrows she painted on every day arched up comically into two points.

I was pretty sure the prospective renters she mentioned didn't exist, but I couldn't call her bluff and risk being homeless in Zumbi until Winkler decided I was important enough to visit. Graciela knew this, meaning a little old Ecuadorian grandmother was successfully extorting $50 out of me for the next couple of months.

After a few days of haggling back and forth, Graciela agreed to let me sign a new contract with her that would raise the rent to $70 (I kicked in ten more dollars than she asked for because it made no difference to me and so she'd shut up about any new bidding wars with imaginary renters). But when I sat down to sign the new contract with her, she changed her mind. Now she wanted $100 a month. I reminded her that I was literally not allowed to pay more than $70, and it was a decision that was out of my hands.

"Okay, okay," she said. "How about $80?"

"Seriously?" I said. "I just told you that I can't pay more than—"

"Here's the thing. If you're not going to pay what that room's really worth, you can't live in it anymore." Mysteriously she was no longer mentioning the alleged seekers willing to pay $60.

"All right, but my boss from Quito won't be visiting me until November. He can approve a new place and the soonest I could move out would be the beginning of December."

Mumbling obscenities under her breath, she agreed and signed the contract. (After I moved out at the end November, no one else ever moved into that room, meaning that by trying to shake me down for the $100 I didn't have, she lost out on $1,330 over the next year and a half.)

From then on, it was war.

I had a place to live until December, but the final three months there were a hellish ordeal full of other extortion attempts. In Graciela's boldest move, she tried blaming me for their rising utilities bill. It had risen from something like eight to twelve dollars a month. The only problem with her hypothesis was that during the month in question, I was out of town for about ten days. Meanwhile, two of her other grandchildren (Consuela's teenaged kids) were in town, one of whom watched TV for no less than eighteen hours a day and frequently left the refrigerator door open. But since I lived in "two rooms" according to Graciela (actually it was just one big one), she screamed and blamed me for the inflated bill.

When she wasn't extorting me, she was tearing my wet laundry down from the clothesline and piling it on the ground or telling me I kept the light on in my room too late or sneaking up on me while I was in the kitchen and telling me I was making toast wrong.

BESIDES CONSUELA, GRACIELA HAD ANOTHER daughter living at the house whose name I never learned. She was mentally handicapped. Graciela restricted her to the confines of their property in the same way—and I truly wince at making this analogy, but it happens to be spot-on—they did with that ogre-looking guy in the movie *The Goonies*. The daughter never said a word to me, or even looked at me, but spent her days wandering around in their yard collecting rocks and muttering violently to herself. I always said hello to her, but she never acknowledged me.

The one time I witnessed this daughter make a move beyond the property and out to the sidewalk, Consuela and Graciela lurched after her yelling, "You don't want us to have to call the police if you wander off, do you? Then we'd have to bring you back and lock you up."

The days and weeks passed and I became somewhat immune to the daily fighting between Graciela and Consuela and the fact that they were both becoming unhinged. They fought about money. They fought about who should discipline Consuela's brat teenagers for not helping around the house. And they fought about the fact that Consuela used Graciela for free babysitting while she went out and partied. (She partied a lot, with lots of men, and the whole town talked about it.) Graciela was upset about the partying in particular; she thought it was no way for a woman in her midthirties—with three kids by three different men, all out of wedlock—to be acting.

While Graciela dealt with me somewhere in between the way she treated her dogs and her handicapped daughter, Consuela was always really nice to me—perhaps even too nice.

Sometime in those first couple of months, I learned that Consuela had a gringo fetish. Before running for city council, she had worked with another Peace Corps volunteer in my province. When the volunteer took her to a meeting in Quito, Consuela got drunk and slept with another young volunteer.

None of this surprised me, but it explained why Winkler came back from his site inspection in Zumbi and told me that the family was eager to have a gringo in the house. He described Consuela as especially "delighted."

Now she would traipse by my bedroom at night wearing nothing but a bath towel, revealing a figure that three births had not been kind to. She'd smile seductively, exposing some missing bicuspids, and ask why I never invited her up to my room.

I smiled and said I liked my privacy.

CHAPTER 25

And then something happened. It was at the time when there was no work for me and Graciela was giving me the stink eye.

During those hot days, I began experiencing a certain pain. It originated in my testicles and ripped through my torso and down my thighs like a lightning bolt. It also shot out from my prostate, reaching deep inside me and clenching every organ and tissue and vessel.

It was true pain.

I felt the first jolt while sitting at a computer in the municipal building and immediately became light-headed and confused. Continuing every hour, then every half hour, the pain pierced and throbbed and ebbed in and out. It came on in surges like a cattle prod had been injected into my veins. When the lightning bolts blasted out from my testicles and prostate (I began calling this my "man plumbing"), I got so nauseated I had to lie down.

After three days of this pain, I put my pride on the back burner and called the Peace Corps doctor in Quito. He asked me all sorts of questions that included words like "shape," "size," "tenderness," and, finally, "discharge." He quickly ruled out the clap because that requires sex, which I wasn't having. (However, this didn't stop people in town from consistently floating rumors that every new baby in town belonged to me. Explaining that I'd been in town just a few months, not nine, did little to convince them otherwise. It got to the point that I was beginning to think that they believed I had some sort of gringo superpower that enabled me to impregnate woman by merely looking at them.)

The doctor told me I had to travel to a nearby town the following day to give a urine sample. That night the air was cool and the town was silent. Too dizzy to read, I lay in bed sweating, my balls throbbing, waiting for the morning to come.

THE FOLLOWING DAY, I TRAVELED twenty minutes by bus to Yantzaza for the urine test. It was strange for two reasons. First, I didn't get to pee into a cup. Instead, I needed pinpoint accuracy to fill a tiny test tube about 1.5 cm in diameter. After I filled it, I had to wash my hands.

Second, the lab technician—a smiling woman in her thirties—had a swastika tattooed on her inner wrist.

This wasn't my first swastika encounter in Ecuador. I'd spotted them carved into chairs, written on the backs of bus seats, and graffitied in alleyways. When I asked people if they knew what the symbol meant, they had no clue, which I guess is slightly less dangerous than knowing and still using it anyway. I attributed the swastika ignorance to the fact that no one around there read books, let alone twentieth-century world-history texts. If most people there couldn't name their previous president, it would be unfair, perhaps, to expect them to know who the Axis was in World War II. Nonetheless, I would have at least Googled the thing before I permanently dyed my skin with it. I decided that the lab technician likely wasn't a Third Reich enthusiast, but if she were, it might explain why—ha, ha—there were no books around.

The lab results said the following: Somewhere deep in my man plumbing was some sort of micro bacteria wreaking havoc. I called the Peace Corps doctor with the results, and he said I should go into the free public health clinic in Zumbi and get a physical exam. The next several days included many calls back and forth between the doctors at my site, me, and the doctor in Quito. Because of Peace

Corps policies, I couldn't see a doctor at site, or anywhere, without permission from the Peace Corps.

All the doctor visits were stressful. I mostly waited around in pain and brushed up on my Spanish medical vocabulary. When it came to dealing with Ecuadorian doctors and my man plumbing, I didn't want anything lost in translation. On the phone with a friend of mine, I said, "Man, I can't believe this dictionary doesn't have the Spanish translation for 'vas deferens.'"

The first local doctor I saw was a beautiful Ecuadorian woman about my age. My conversation with her was brief because she said I had to come back after the weekend and see a specialist who wouldn't be in until Monday. She sent me on my way with some ibuprofen and instructed me to take 1,200 milligrams a day for relief.

It didn't help. Over the weekend, I writhed in pain and boredom. The only times I left my bedroom were to briefly go downstairs to the kitchen and bring some food back to my room, where I lay in bed sweating and moaning. On Sunday, I lay there late into the day until I heard violent noises down on the patio. I rolled out of bed and hobbled to the window to find Jack and Benji snarling in an intense dogfight. Jack was about to rip Benji's head off. Blood was spurting from Benji and covering Jack's muzzle.

Just then Graciela stormed out of the kitchen wielding a broomstick. She began beating Jack so hard that the broomstick snapped in half. She picked up the broken end and kept beating him with it. When the fight finally broke up, she dragged Jack over to his usual post and tied him up, then beat him some more and started filling the washbasin with water. It looked like she might be getting ready to drown Jack to death. I'd seen some grisly mammalian slaughters in my half year there, but I never imagined I'd see an old lady finish off a snarling dog with her bare hands.

Instead, she threw buckets of water at Jack and began beating him again. Later, I suggested to Consuela—for about the tenth time— that they should just train Jack to be a little nicer. She just laughed, as usual, and said, "No, he's just bad," which, ironically, is the same thing she'd told me earlier about her five-year-old son who'd had problems acting out.

ON MONDAY THE SPECIALIST GAVE me a checkup with what might have been the only pair of latex gloves in the building. Before the exam, he left the room to look for them and returned minutes later wiggling his fingers in the air in triumph. The doctors here, I decided, weren't all that bad. It was just the facilities that made you want to shower immediately.

The specialist prescribed some antibiotics in pill form as well as more ibuprofen and a heavy medicine that would be injected. Also, he said, I needed to go to Loja for a more thorough exam.

"What kind of exam will it be?" I said.

"An ultrasound."

"Excuse me?"

"An ultrasound," he said. "Like they do on pregnant women—"

"Ah, yes, I know what it is—"

"—except on your testicles."

He stood up and told me there was one last thing I could do to ease the pain. He said I should fill a bowl with hot water and soak my testicles in it—yes, just like a teabag. In an up and down motion, flexing his knees, he stood in front of me and demonstrated exactly how I could go about dipping my testicles in the bowl.

I let this sink in, then got on the phone to run it all by the Peace Corps doctor.

"Ummm, yeah, Grigs, this is all good. Take the antibiotics for ten days. You can buy it at a local pharmacy," said the Peace Corps doctor.

"Okay. And this one that's supposed to be injected? What's that all about?" I said.

"Oh, right. To buy that one, go to the next town over—for political purposes."

"*Political purposes?*" I said.

"Right, well, it's like this: Even though you don't have an STD, that medicine is sometimes also used for patients who do. Therefore . . . just so you don't have any gossip swirling around your town, go and buy that medicine somewhere else."

"Oh," I said. "Good idea."

Before going in for the shot, I went back to my house to rest. Not only was I sapped of energy, but I also had to mentally psyche myself up for what was looking like a large injection.

While taking my temperature (I was also battling a terrible fever), I dropped my thermometer on the floor, emitting a mercury spill upon impact. This sent me into a small panic until I realized I was already getting a healthy dose of mercury in the tuna I bought there, which probably wasn't dolphin safe in the first place. I cleaned up the Hg the best I could and returned to the doctor's office.

When I arrived, word had already spread that the gringo was going to receive a shot. As three doctors and several nurses crowded into a room, I lay on a cot, pale-faced and drenched in sweat. There was no translation in my dictionary for "vasovagal."

Into the room came the beautiful young doctor from the week before.

"You don't look too good," she said, smiling.

"I don't do well with injections," I said.

A few of the nurses turned around; they all asked what I was talking about.

"You know," I said. "I get dizzy when I receive injections. I lose color in my face." (This last sentence almost certainly didn't translate the way that I'd hoped.)

"That's weird."

"You've never seen anybody who didn't do well with injections?" I said.

"Tons of ladies come in here from the *campo* and they're just fine," they all said.

"Well," I said, "this is something that happens with gringos."

"Aha," they all said, nodding to one another like they'd finally gotten to the bottom of this mystery.

The young doctor leaned over to my left arm to administer the shot.

Before she pricked me, I said, "You guys use brand-new needles, right? Totally clean and everything?" By now even my limbs had lost all color and I could barely keep my eyes open. My heart was pounding in my ears and I felt like I was going to faint.

"Oh yes," they all said. The doctor showed me the package that had contained the needle.

After a few minutes of the hot doctor slowly injecting me, she uttered that she'd "lost the vein" because I was "too nervous." She said maybe someone else should do it.

Another nurse took over and the medicine was finally injected. Some color returned to my arms and hands. I got a free Band-Aid. I staggered out and went home. For the next couple of days, I continued to live in seclusion in my bedroom, only telling people that I "wasn't feeling great."

I SPENT THE REST OF that week not working—or even leaving the house—and secretly bringing pots of stove-heated water from the kitchen outside and up to my room for the scrotum soakings. Graciela spotted me carrying the water once or twice and looked at me suspiciously, but never asked for details.

Three days later, I went to Loja for the nut ultrasound. With the lightning bolts of pain still striking out from my testicles and prostate, it was one of the longest three-hour bus rides of my life.

This time, as I lay on an exam table with my shorts pulled down below my thighs, I actually began laughing. Even as the pain continued with me lying there, I laughed maniacally at what I'd gone through. The doctor covered my scrotum with the same clear gel that normally gets smeared onto pregnant bellies. I held a towel in place to keep my penis out of the way of the ultrasound wand.

The first thing the doctor did on the computer was derive all my testicles' statistics, including mass, density, circumference, diameter, and volume. During the course of the ultrasound, the doctor took several sonogram portraits of my testicular topography. A few of them looked like black-and-white Doppler shots you might see on the Weather Channel—a Category Four storm brewing somewhere between Bermuda and Nassau. After the exam, he printed out the results—the images and nut stats—on a giant sheet of x-ray paper. I'm not much of a collector, but I quickly decided it was by far my best travel souvenir.

It turned out that some pesky jungle bacteria had worked its way through my man plumbing and lodged in the spermatic cord. In the sonogram I could actually see the bacteria clogging up the thin cord attaching my left testicle to the rest of my body. Just the picture of that replaces all adequate descriptions I could give for the pain originating in this part of my body. The doctor said the infection was small enough that instead of surgery, I could continue blasting it with antibiotics like Cipro, which I began taking every day. Beyond that, he said, there was nothing to be alarmed about.

I left Loja while the sun was setting. By the time we got close to Zumbi, it was dark out and I could see the lights from town as we wound down the road. The bus was packed; I was crammed in a window seat, with my face nearly squished against the glass, clutching the x-ray paper in my hand. The combination of the lights of Zumbi shining on the other side of the river and the pictures of my balls in the manila envelope seemed to highlight my loneliness. Tired and pissed off, I felt a tear roll down my cheek. *Aha, my first Peace Corps tear*, I thought. There in the bus—manila envelope, lights of Zumbi, clenched prostate, throbbing balls—I felt the tear crawl down my face nice and slow. I let it hang there as I looked out the window into the night. And then I wiped it away and said to myself—actually *said* it aloud—"Stop being a pussy."

In the week that followed, the pain receded. The Peace Corps doctor said in addition to the spermatic cord infection, it might have also developed into a prostatitis, which explained the sphincter-clenching agony that resulted when the lightning bolts of pain seemed to originate not just from my testicles, but also from the deepest recesses of my man plumbing.

The diagnosis came toward the end of an eight-week period in which I was dangerously depressed.

CHAPTER 26

While the pain continued and I was in Zumbi alone with no work to do, I would lie in bed and become infuriated with everything around me. I hated Ecuador—this disgusting, pitiful country that had put me in so much pain. I hated it for what it had done to me in such a short time. It had nearly crushed me. Everything from my old site boiled up and ruined me inside. When I'd first shared the story with friends, an abduction attempt in the desert wastelands had seemed thrilling. But now the hideous nature of it all got to me. It gave me nightmares and crept up on me while I was awake and left me cursing the assholes I'd met there who treated my well-being as carelessly as they treated everything else in their pathetic lives.

Those motherfuckers, I would think, as I clenched my teeth and my fists. I fantasized about someday telling those people what I really thought of them after I'd stayed quiet like an abused child, bottling it up day after day because I was scared of the consequences. I pictured going to La Segua on my last day in the country and doing something fantastically violent to each and every one of them.

Now, months after leaving that place, I would receive vaguely threatening phone calls on a weekly basis from the coastal scumbags. I thought about changing my number, but there was something exciting and menacing about answering the calls and holding my palm over the receiver as Juan's friends and relatives shouted obscenities and also truisms like "I know you're there."

Some of the numbers I resaved in my phone as "xxx" instead of a name so I'd know not to answer it anymore. Sometimes they called rapid fire, twenty times in a minute, as I struggled to press END as quickly as they came in. Or they'd call from a number I had made the mistake of deleting, so I'd pick up and say hello in my gringo accent only to hear "Aha, motherfucker! We know it's you. Motherfucking son of a bitch!" on the other end. I used to stay on the line listening in silence to the threats with the same arousal kids get by ringing a doorbell and hiding in the bushes to observe the neighbor yell in anger from his porch. With my silence, I tried to drag the calls on as long as possible. I wanted to burn away the precious minutes they were always so scant on that they begged to borrow my phone. Take that!

One day they gave up and the calls ceased, but my solitary war of anger raged on. I felt like South America—the land I loved so much that at one time I'd felt *part* of it—had done this to me.

And here I am now, I thought, *angry and all alone.*

The thought that this country was worthy of receiving my help filled me with sinister and self-loathing laughter.

I was angry with the Peace Corps. How do you send some volunteers to frolic in the rainforest or mangroves with good organizations while you send others to work with a Napoleon-complexed child in a community resembling an open-air insane asylum?

The anger exploded from every one of my pores.

How does your boss in the office, stammering on the other end of the phone, tell you these "misunderstandings" are "common" and then try to convince the country director to keep you out there? I envisioned walking into his office on my last day in this despicable country and telling him what I thought of him, too: "Your job is to help me but you did the opposite because you didn't want extra paperwork. You put me in danger because you forgot I'm a human and not just a name on a piece of paper."

My blood boiled more as I strolled through Zumbi with nothing to do. I'd pass the FODI people I worked with for all of two months and they'd ask me, inexplicably, if I'd still been going into the office. I explained that neither they nor anyone else was *in* the office. I wanted to scream in their face that they didn't have any work for me to do even when they were actually employed there.

And then I'd go back to burning with rage over how I got sent there. How could Winkler have pawned me off on this community to work with government-paid babysitters who only wanted a gringo they could flirt with?

Winkler had acted like it was the worst inconvenience he'd ever faced to come down to my site and see if they still wanted another volunteer, all while I sat on my ass in Quito for nearly two weeks. The result of his haste was that he chose the worst host family possible.

Graciela became more crazed by the day. And Consuela kept flirting with me and would *just happen* to walk through the kitchen seminude at odd hours of the day when I was eating alone. The idea repulsed me and further entrenched me in the solitary confinement of my bedroom—my cocoon of hatred.

I also stewed at my family back home. On one hand, I'd hated their response to the incident in Manabí: Some told me to quit and come home. On the other hand, my spears of hatred hurled their way for not *understanding* what I now realized: that being here was all a sick mistake. I was pissed at them for thinking I could get through it. *You weren't here*, I thought. *You didn't have to be around those people like I did.* Eventually I gave up on trying to relay any more feelings or descriptions their way. The anger would hurt them. The loneliness would frighten them. There really is nothing lonelier than anger being thrown in all directions.

Now, Winkler was assaulting me with manic emails and phone calls about Reconnect, the Peace Corps meeting where we had to show up with our counterparts and give presentations explaining what we'd discovered in our interviews and analyses of our communities in the first few months.

"What do you mean you don't have anyone from your community to bring to the meeting?" he barked.

"Well, everyone you sent me here to work with has been fired," I calmly explained. "Just as you predicted."

He'd chortle and come back with something like, "Well, this just won't do."

His calls and emails became increasingly frantic and devastating for my mood. I'd invited everyone in my town I could think of, including my former coworkers. They all said no. They said it sounded stupid, to which I had no effective reply.

In a sign of just how unsettling Winkler's calls were becoming, I'd even committed the potentially disastrous maneuver of asking Consuela to come. She was, after all, an important political figure in town. I knew she'd say no and she did—she was busy touring around the county on political business—though I'm sure she managed to mistake my invitation as some sort of signal, which led to more nausea-inducing come-ons from her every day when we passed each other. (One day while I was eating breakfast alone in the kitchen, she came in wearing only a bra and short workout shorts. She pointed out to me how hard she was trying to lose weight by only drinking smoothies and how she just needed someone to massage her midsection like so to allow the rolls of billowing flesh to tighten up. I believe she was fishing for a compliment, so I told her she looked good, not wanting to hurt her feelings. She eventually left the room, but I'd lost my appetite.)

The frequency of Winkler's calls and the despair in his voice started giving me more anxiety than the threatening calls from the animals at my old site. His calls ended with him saying, "Please, *please*, we just *can't* have you show up to the meeting alone." I was beginning to think showing up solo to this thing was the Peace Corps equivalent of career suicide.

In the second week of September, after traveling seventeen hours on a bus, I finally arrived in Puyo for the big event. At the meeting, more than half the other volunteers had no counterpart.

CHAPTER 27

Toward the end of October, the testicular pain that had momentarily waned staged a forceful comeback. When the cattle prod-like jolts of pain again became too much to take, I called the Peace Corps doctor.

Now I needed to go all the way to Quito to get checked out by some specialists, he said. The trip would probably include another ultrasound in addition to other exams. The following week, I took the fifteen-hour bus ride.

On the trip from Loja to Quito, I sat next to another volunteer who was leaving her site and Early Terminating. She was throwing in the towel after about three months at her site. She said she didn't like the community. She hadn't had any incidents, but she said she felt unsafe and uncomfortable. She asked me why I was going to Quito and I told her. We said no more and both slept for the rest of the ride.

I got to Quito at 7 a.m. By 11:30 a.m. I was naked in the fetal position on the exam table of an internal medicine specialist named Dr. Mendez. His office was inside a private hospital in northern Quito—by far the nicest medical building I'd ever been in. Dr. Mendez wanted to get to the bottom of my unusual amount of pain.

First he ruled out a torsion (which is kind of like a game of tetherball between your testicles). Next he administered a prostate exam. Holding up his index finger inside a latex glove, he said in perfect

English, "If this is merely uncomfortable, your prostate is fine; if it's painful, we'll need another exam." He wiggled his finger and I let out a whimper. He concluded that I had some combination of epididymitis and prostatitis. Just to confirm it, the next morning I would return to the clinic for my second testicular ultrasound. As a bonus, I would roll over for a rectal sonogram right afterward.

I left Dr. Mendez's office and walked up the street to the Peace Corps headquarters. Once there, I stopped by Winkler's office to say hello. I sat down for a few minutes, squirming in the chair as the bolts of pain tore through my body and he bitched at me for not having an official counterpart. I told him I was working on it. His griping made me a bit dizzy so I said we'd talk later and walked over to the doctor's office.

The doctor asked me how the consultation with Mendez went. I told him.

"Well, how you feeling, man?" he asked.

"All right, I guess," I said. "That's the first finger in the butt I've gotten from a doctor."

"Yeah, no fun, dude," he said. "Well, let's get you ready for the rectal ultrasound tomorrow. You doing okay?"

"Sure," I said.

"How about your pride?"

We both laughed.

In preparation for the test the next morning, he handed me some laxatives and told me to take them that night.

"One more thing," he said. "Have you ever done an enema?"

"No."

He handed me the prescription paper.

"When do we have to do it?" I asked.

"Oh no, you're going to administer this one yourself, man."

"When?"

"Um, hold on . . ." he pulled up the WebMD website on his computer. "Seven in the morning."

"Okay."

"And, Grigs, don't squeeze it in too fast because it can have a nauseating effect."

My alarm went off at 6 a.m., and I used the next hour to get myself mentally ready for the self-administered enema. The squishy plastic bottle with its nozzle like a hummingbird's beak had been on the nightstand staring me down all night. The directions on the box were in Spanish with drawn diagrams: There were two options for how I could go about this.

The first option required a doggy-style position, which seemed to have no amount of dignity to it. I chose the second, which involved taking the pose of the inside person of a couple that is "spooning." The directions then called for you to use one arm to pull your knees closer to your chest while using your other arm to reach around behind and . . .

THE SPERMATIC CORD WAS NO longer infected, but the rest of the testicular ultrasound and the (harrowing) rectal ultrasound were inconclusive. So after a trip to Quito and multiple things getting shoved up my ass, I still didn't have any real answers on how to ease the pain. In addition to having me continue with the Cipro, Dr. Mendez prescribed Celebrex, making me probably the first person under the age of fifty to take said drug.

On Sunday evening I took an overnight bus back to Loja. I stayed in Loja Monday night to watch the Denver Broncos on *Monday Night Football*. I was back in site Tuesday morning and went a solid week without nut pain.

CHAPTER 28

But of course the pain returns and I'm back in Zumbi and the time is passing . . .

A man in Zumbi builds a cockfighting coliseum in his backyard, and even for an animal lover, it's a pretty fun way to spend a Saturday afternoon of drinking. These guys take their cock fighting seriously. The entire time I watch, I contemplate the moral ambiguity of my participation . . .

I take more long bus trips across the country to see friends and attend conferences for volunteers. I pass through most of the provinces. I ride by every volcano, through every big city, on every major highway. I stare out the window, gazing at the wide-open spaces. And I think about all the things that people typically think about when they stare off into those wide-open spaces . . .

Here I am sitting on the bus next to Ecuadorians who strike up conversations with some of the weirdest questions I could ever think of: do we eat rice in the United States, have I tasted beer before, how much does my shirt cost, how much money do I make, how much does my hat cost, how much does my backpack cost, how much does my iPod cost, how many kids do I have.

And here I am with these passengers who badger me with statements like, "There's no vegetation in the U.S., is there? No, there isn't. Ha! Plants? Animals? You don't have any of it. Ha! Not like here.

Ecuador—we have the most natural beauty on the face of the earth. It's true!" Then they say excuse me so they can reach across me and dump their trash out the window. The first dozen times, this leads to a conversation about the ails of litter. But after that I don't have the patience for it anymore . . .

Here I am, as usual, spending the night alone in my apartment, soaking my balls in a bowl of warm water . . .

Here I am waking up on Sundays in Zumbi to such quiet and empty streets that I wonder if everyone moved out of town overnight and didn't warn me about it . . .

Here I am buying groceries from the corner store and coming face-to-face with the status of Ecuadorian gender roles. "What—are you planning on *cooking something*?" the woman behind the counter says in a mocking tone, like I could only have some vague idea of what it takes to work in a kitchen . . .

Here I am making an addition to a daily journal I've been keeping since I arrived. Whereas before, it just had a few words describing where I was and what I did on a particular day, now I noted my testicular and prostatic pain. So instead of "Zumbi: talk with neighbor," it would now say something like "Zumbi: morning, dull throbbing; afternoon, piercing feeling" . . .

And here's Graciela barging into my room one day to ask me to lend her twenty dollars. The glorious part is that I actually don't have any money on me because the ATM machine in the next town over hasn't been working. Graciela looks me in the eye and says, "Liar. Of course you have money. All of you have money." And she waddles out of the room shaking her head . . .

There are landslides on the only road leading out of the province to Loja—that winding deathtrap of a road that they've been trying to pave since I arrived in Zumbi. Rocks fall. People die. Traffic stops. And after five days without passage, Zumbi and nearby towns are running out of food and not receiving newspapers and the only topic of conversation all day long is the status of the road . . .

Older volunteers leave and newer ones arrive. The volunteer who lives a few hours east of me requests that a new volunteer replace him when he's gone. I ask why, since he spent his two years struggling to get any projects going. His answer is that he wants his host family to keep receiving the rent money ("They *need* that income," he says). A new volunteer eventually arrives in that site and lives . . . in a different house . . .

Shortly thereafter, I take steps to make sure the Peace Corps does *not* put any new volunteers in my site unless there is a foundation or group that specifically has a job for them to do . . .

And here are more emails and texts from Winkler making random threats of Administrative Separation for offenses like not properly texting him our whereabouts . . .

Here I am playing in Zumbi's municipal basketball league (and eventually letting the municipality make false worker documents for me so I can be on their all-star team and compete against other teams around the province). Zumbi's gym is actually an impressive structure, with a full-sized court and seating room for a few hundred, all covered by a tin roof. I am a head taller than everyone else on the court and after just one game in the league, I feel like Kobe Bryant— I *am* Kobe Bryant. Every time I touch the ball I know I will score. It's a marvelous feeling. Players on other teams try tackling me and stage complaints to the referees that I—who haven't played organized basketball since the seventh grade—am "too good" and that it's "unfair." Ecuadorian basketball brings out the worst in all of us, including me. I eventually am a magnet for technical fouls when I decide to point out to the ref that the other team jumping on my back and trying to trip me are, by any standard definition, fouls. When the ref is unmoved by my complaints, I swear in English, prompting more technical fouls and causing all my teammates to harass the ref for the rest of the game with, "Oh, smart guy here thinks he speaks English now. Ha!" My basketball career in Ecuador ends when I sprain my ankle in the opening minutes of the municipal league's championship game. With the entire town watching, I play through it, we lose by one point, and the ankle bothers me for the next seven months . . .

In October 2009 the indigenous groups go on strike to protest new laws that, among other things, would extract more water and minerals and petroleum from the Amazonian provinces. They block major roads with boulders and burning tires, effectively paralyzing the country for about a week. In jungle towns to the north of me, skirmishes break out between Shuar political leaders and the military, resulting in deaths. The Peace Corps puts volunteers on Stand Fast, meaning we can't leave our sites until further notice. (Other times we'd been put on Stand Fast included national Election Day and a short period of time months earlier when the swine flu hysteria first hit.) During this Stand Fast, one volunteer I don't know very well sends a text message to his friend saying that they will leave their sites, meet up in a big city nearby, and—using some crude terms to describe a vagina—will be, um, meeting females. But he doesn't send it to his friend; he sends it to the Peace Corps country director, whose cell phone number was apparently listed too close to his friend's name in his contacts list. The volunteer is not a member of Peace Corps Ecuador much longer . . .

Near the end of the year, our country director resigns. In addition to making the correct decision to pull me out of La Segua before things got worse, she was kind and smart and professional. A lot of other volunteers had a bizarre distrust of her because she herself had never been a volunteer. After she leaves, others in the Quito office label her a dictator. But I liked her. Two interim directors follow before our new country director arrives . . .

CHAPTER 29

Over the Halloween weekend, three other volunteers and I traveled north to Cuenca. We left our sites on a Thursday afternoon. Our plan was to wake up Friday at another volunteer's house located in the mountains outside the city and do San Pedro, a cactus that grows in the northern Andes and contains the psychedelic chemical mescaline. On Saturday, we would head back down into Cuenca to celebrate Halloween with dozens of other volunteers in the city.

The trip got off to a strange start. As I got on the bus at the Loja station, I was pickpocketed. In all my previous travels, the closest I'd come to being hurt or robbed in any way involved getting chased down a street by a gang of transvestites in a bad part of Buenos Aires at 5 a.m.

This was the first time anyone had ever stolen from me.

After the initial flush of panic and frustration over the violation, I realized this was likely the least successful larceny operation in modern history: Not only was my cell phone in the opposite pocket, untouched, but my ATM card was also safe and sound in another pocket. A hundred dollars in cash was stuffed in my shoe. My important documents were hidden away in other secure locations. All that was gone was my wallet, which had $1.60 and an expired credit card in it. But the best part was that the stolen wallet had Che Guevara's famous image emblazoned on the front (because whoever designed it understood marketing but not irony).

We got to the volunteer's house outside Cuenca after nightfall. She was there with another friend. The house sat on a giant piece of property that was fenced in toward the street and opened up to a view of a giant sweeping valley out back. The next day we prepared the San Pedro. First we had to peel the cactus and take out the pulp that was closest to the outer skin. When we skinned enough of it, we sat around for hours, waiting for the cactus parts to boil down into a putrid black tea. All six of us were going to do it. I hardly knew any of them; they were volunteers who'd been in Ecuador longer than I had and treated me the way high school seniors treat freshmen.

The first time I did San Pedro was two and a half years before, outside Cuzco. It was the most beautiful experience of my life. And it had been a year and a half since I'd eaten psilocybin mushrooms with my two best friends from college and lain on our living room floor thinking I had figured out the purpose of life.

Now I was nervous.

We drank the awful tasting tea around 4:30 p.m.

An hour later I felt it.

Chills set in. I wrapped myself in a large blanket and sat outside staring off over the valley. The last rays of light pierced through the clouds and glowed orange and red out over the butte. Earlier in the day the power had gone out in the area, so the valley quickly darkened as the sun set.

I found scrap wood and built a fire. I watched the flames alone. Then four of the others came over giggling like hyenas. I returned to my chair and stared out across the valley for a bit. I put on my iPod and played Ennio Morricone's theme to *Once Upon a Time in the West*. It was around eight o'clock and the sky was dark purple.

The pure pitched voice sang in my ears. Clouds rolled over. I was cold but I inhaled and a blissful warmth filled my lungs and torso. Ahhhhhhhhh. As the song reached a crescendo, the electricity came back on, illuminating tiny sparkles across the valley in a wave that seemed nothing short of miraculous. It nearly brought tears to my eyes; I applauded and laughed hysterically. The others asked what was happening. I explained. They stayed around the fire I'd built making stupid jokes. When they came over to sit by me, I felt claustrophobic.

HERE, TONIGHT, I LOOK AROUND at the five other people and there is no common wavelength. First, see them dancing around the fire making comments like, "Dude, bro, I'm tripping *balls*." See them gyrate and give high-fives because of a hysterical burp. Or make potty jokes and erupt into tears-in-the-eyes laughter. Or insist on watching a bootlegged DVD of *America's Funniest Home Videos* and make comments like, "Dude, that's the most awesome pet cat I've ever seen."

And then comes the most terrifying, soul-scratching feeling of them all (as the chemicals slip deeper into my bodily tissues): that the people I have chosen to share this mind-altering psychedelic occasion with are . . . not funny.

So do I sit and close my eyes and ponder space and the incomprehensible beauty of life and soak it all in?

No. I freak out.

I get up to take a walk around the property. I get some water and come back.

It doesn't feel right.

I go get some more water.

It still doesn't feel right.

I go back inside the house where the others are now lying down.

"I'm not doing too well," I say.

No answers.

"I mean really, I'm just all of a sudden having a bad time here," I say. They all stare at me with dark, judging eyes.

"What do you want us to do?" one of them says, his words spilling out all at once.

"I don't know. I think I just need some comfort. I'm going to lie down."

The one who kept announcing earlier that he was "tripping balls" stands up and looks at me for a second. "Dude," he says, "just chill out. We're all tripping out of our minds too. Just . . . whatever."

Everyone laughs. "Yeahhh, man," a couple of them say. "Whatever."

"Yeah."

"Dude."

I lie down by a floor heater and stare up at the ceiling and the clock on the wall.

At 9:15, the true terror sets in. It is true, Satan-scratching-at-your-doorstep fury—a spiral of paranoia.

You're losing your mind.

The woman whose house we were in, Katie, offers me milk. She is, and always was, kind.

"This is going to end sometime, right?"

"Yeah," she says. "You'll be fine."

"I think I just have to remind myself that," I said. "Ehhhhhh Ahhhhhhh. Oh fuck." The noise lurches uncontrollably from somewhere deep in my chest.

I go outdoors and puke. I try to puke everything that's in my belly, even the bile. The vomit piles up next to the woodpile by the tool shed. I have to pee, so I do that too—on top of the pile of vomit. I venture back indoors and lie down by the heater. Something evil still scratches away at me.

My torso is in pain, like all the pain I've ever felt in my life is clawing to get out of there. The terror and dread come on heavy like another growl.

I'm not coming out of this. Losing things. No comfort.

I close my eyes and a giant snake leaps toward me. Its skin is shiny and metallic and all different colors. It tries to swallow me whole. I tell it no, with an evil giggle.

Oh god, what a mistake.

"I'll get through this," I say out loud.

Then I whisper under my breath, "I'm here now." I close my eyes and open them again.

Something screams at me, WHY DO YOU FEEL THIS WAY, HUH. There are no question marks. These are not questions.

Like vrooooooooooommmmmm powwwwwwwwwwww, there's a beast escaping from my stomach. I growl and let it out. *That giant scary serpent better never come back, I'll make sure of it.*

I want to cry, thinking it's a way of getting rid of the demon. *What a pussy.*

"Ooohhhahahhaeeeeeeeeehhhhhhhhggrrrrrrrrrr." A growl comes out of me again.

YOU STOP IT.

You're a monster.

People doubting me. People laughing at me. No one gets it. Space travel. Bicycle rides.

I am here now. This will pass. It's 9:35. This will pass. I am Grigs. This is me, this will pass. I will be all better in a few hours. Don't panic. Stay calm. I will NOT fucking panic. There is no panicking here. No panicking!

Heart leaping from my chest. Pain coming from everywhere.

While this pain is making its way out, I may as well let it all out.

I announce that the pain in my nuts is going away forever. (Not, as it turns out, true.) Another howl through the night and I'm dripping in sweat.

Just wish I had someone here who understands me. Someone I love. Someone who loves me. Someone who doesn't doubt me. Someone to hold me.

WHAT ARE YOU SCARED OF? ARE YOU SCARED IT'S NEVER GOING TO END?

Please, please, PLEASE. Go away.

WHAT THE FUCK ARE YOU DOING HERE?

I'm just living. Growing. Leave me alone.

NOBODY LOVES YOU.

You are losing your mind.

YOU ARE LOSING YOUR MIND.

I am losing my mind.

My family loves me, I'm sure of it. This will pass and I'll look back on this and be proud of myself that I climbed out of this darkness.

AT SIXTEEN YOU BEGAN BEING DEPRESSED. HOW PATHETIC. NOW YOU'RE TWENTY-THREE. TIME TO GROW UP.

Time to grow up.

TIME TO GROW UP.

I'm sorry. I'm trying.

YOU FEEL LIKE A BLACK SHEEP, DON'T YOU.

None of that's real. All stuff made up in my head. Somewhere else.

"Yeeeeeeeeeooooooooowwwwwwwwwwww. Ahhhhhhhhh."

I remember the time I lost a small red shovel in the ocean and the surf carried it away. I remember Topanga. I remember running around dressed like an Indian. I remember my first pet dog.

I feel my life and it feels like a tin can being scraped across the sidewalk. The soul is drifting farther and farther away and getting scratched more across the pavement. And then . . .

Skiing in the pure silence. Christmas mornings. Your grandmother reading everything you ever wrote and saying she loved it and thinking you had talent. All your doggies cuddling with you on the couch. Catch-22. Elephants. Bulls. Penguins. The end of the world—no, the tip of the continent. Argentina. You felt at home in Buenos Aires. You felt connected. You remember waking up in the hospital with your mom by your side holding your hand and her looking very sad. Getting wheeled down the hospital hallway. The kid in the next room having seizures. A friend bringing you a big stuffed cow. You've got the scars all over you. You're proud of them, aren't you. You'd be nothing without them. Being underwater. Swimming out at the golf club in the California desert. Climbing Longs Peak. Lewis and Clark expedition. Monticello. You remember when you were little, lying there in the top bunk during the earthquake. The fires. The mudslides. Rainy days when you were a kid. A house burns down. Visiting the Middle East with your brother. A sandstorm. North Carolina. Barbeques. Northern Michigan in the summer. Making mistakes with people's hearts. Shooting a shotgun and feeling the strange jolt. First kiss. First real kiss. First fuck. First real fuck. Going back and doing things over. Favorite colors. Pirates off the coast of Mexico. Mayan ruins. The dream when you were little about Captain Hook taking you away in a wheel barrow. Blood streaming down your arm. Being a scapegoat. Being the class clown. Everyone laughing at you. People not forgiving you. People blaming you. All the women you've ever had sex with.

You remember driving to Graceland. Graceland. You remember the wind blowing through the windows between Nashville and Memphis. Graceland. You remember Sun Studios. Graceland. You remember Tupelo and Birmingham. Graceland. You remember the jungle room. Yes: Graceland.

You remember the English professor in college who stood in front of your class in a tweed jacket and said, "Someday you'll look yourself in the mirror and realize that one day you're going to die. And it's a strange feeling."

You remember talking to your friend about Hemingway and how he said, "I challenge you to find one story of his that isn't about death." And you keep on looking.

The spiral of terror comes and goes.

Oh man oh man, oh my, don't lose your fucking mind. You're smarter than this. Don't lose it all.

Landslides of thought.

Take a deep breath and it swells the belly full. Feels good. Exhale and rub like a satisfied bear.

YOU'RE BITTER, AREN'T YOU. It rasps at me.

I'm so sorry. Is this ruining my brain? No, I'll be back. This is scary.

I get inside a sleeping bag that Katie lent me for the night. It's warm in there. I love that warmth. Second best thing next to comfort—the warmth.

I can't find any comfort with these people here. I've got to get it on my own. A beast of pain leaves my torso in an outward rushing funnel of bad energy.

Take the bad energy and turn it into good. Do it, now. Flip it up-side down like a giant pendulum swinging vertically. Flip it. That's what you're supposed to do.

I yell more and announce that I'm getting rid of the pain. I am pushing the pain out of my nuts forever. The pain doesn't stand a chance. None of it. The tears still won't come.

This is cruel and unusual.

You're losing control. Reel everything in your life back in.

TAKE CONTROL.

Love.

YOU ARE LOSING YOUR MIND.

I am losing my mind.

The soul has left the body. It might come back. "Rahhhhhhhh-hhhhhhhhhhh zooooooooooommmmmmmmm!"

YES. IT'S ALL TRUE.

Someone from across the room: "Grigs, man what do you want to talk about that would cheer you up?"

"Tom Wolfe."

"Who the hell is Tom Wolfe?" They all laugh like hyenas sucking on helium.

Philistines! Fuck!

Darkness. Vines. Washington, D.C. Amsterdam. Africa. Ocean liner. Oil. Dictators. Bananas. Mustaches. All the mouths you've ever kissed. All the drinks you've ever drunk. All the steaks you've ever sliced. All the sidewalks you've walked. All the swear words you've ever said. All the people you've hurt. All the times you've cried. When was the last time? Crying in the shower in high school. Crying in the middle of the night in college. Crying in a therapist's office and not wanting to talk about it. Feeling it bottle up in the bottom of your throat. A girl touching her hand to my chest and feeling it go down down down. Golfing. Driving to the mountains. Crossing the border. Cormac McCarthy. Seagulls. Natural History Museums. IMAX films. Wind chimes making you feel lonely. Hot tubs in the snow. The view of earth shot from the moon. Launching into outer space.

A million more thoughts. It goes on and on, motherfucker. Yeeeeessssssssssssssssssss . . .

Eric Clapton's autobiography. Bob Dylan's autobiography. My autobiography. Bill Clinton. Kofi Annan. Cape Coast. Magellan. Apollo. Zeus. Corsica. Portugal. Sailboats. White. Deep blue. Bright orange. Blood red. Pitch black. Mustard yellow. Hot. Cold. Drowning. Planting a root. Twenty years. Twenty three and a half years. And what have you done. People who don't know what you're going through. What you've been through. Where you've been. The places you're going. People always disagreeing with you. Whale watching. Polar bears in the zoo. Lawrence of Arabia. East Asia. Long ropes. Medicines for pain. Medicines for the cold. Medicines for malaria. Medicines for pain in the balls. Doctors with pens in their pockets. Doctors sliding across the floor on wheeled chairs. Love at first sight. Yossarian. Britain. Twisted ankles. Playing baseball in the heat. Not getting strikes called. Teachers telling you that you'll be successful. A teacher on the playground saying you were a bad kid. Having to tell a teacher why you missed the exam when you were too depressed to get out of bed. Missing your ride to school. Planes crashing into buildings. Fuel-efficient cars. Politicians. Liars. Newscasters. Cheaters. Brains colliding inside helmets. Dairy Queen. Strawberry-banana smoothies. The Alamo. Mount Rushmore. Newport. Florida. Crows. Thanksgivings with family. The giant willow tree in the backyard. The Red Hot Chili Peppers. Van Morrison. Mowing the lawn in the morning and the way the cut grass smelled. A fly buzzing over your head when you wake up. A guitar that feels great in your hands. Naked bodies. People embarrassed of themselves. People being self-conscious. Orchestral music. Plays. Stand-up comedy. Dressing up in a suit. The time your grandpa looked at your mom and called her his baby girl and you smiled to think that she was still somebody's baby. The elephant painting. Wild tusks. Whoooooooooooooooooo.

ARE YOU STILL SCARED.

Not so much. It's slowing down.

YES IT IS. AND YOU'RE GOING TO MISS IT.

This is just a time and I'll get through it.

You don't even know if you're talking about this instant or something bigger.

Maybe it's one and the same.

IT'S SLOWING DOWN.

A little bit of bliss comes on.

It's 10:45. The darkest part is over. I feel embarrassed and self-conscious. All these people think I'm some sort of freak.

Still a million thoughts. I kinda feel empty. I kinda feel sorry. I kinda feel glad and happy. I'm not even sure what happened.

I thank Katie for bringing me the milk. "This is true. You understand people. You understand things."

The belts and axles that make a car go are slowing down in my head. The film reel of images is slowing down. Sighs of relief. The big machine in the sky is turning off.

Listen to some Kings of Leon. Some Gershwin. Some Tom Petty. Let it wash over you and cool you down. Eat a bagel. Drink some juice. Rub your toes together for a couple of hours straight. Lay on your side. Keep your eyes away from the TV screen. Block out all the hideous laughter. Exhale deeply. Ignore everything else. Take off your shirt so your chest can feel the coolness. Lights are off all around now. No one else understands the music but it's okay. Close your eyes and know that love is somewhere around you. Somewhere in you. The thoughts are slowing down and you're taking them where you want to take them. You're getting through this. Good job. You fought like a lion. Ohhhhh. Remember the Roman Coliseum. Ahhhhh. Sweetness. Milk and honey. Parades. Spring season. Let it all out. Freud. All your kind professors. A bar where you can drink a gin and tonic and hear yourself think. Love is—yes, it's all around; maybe not right here right now, but you're never far from it.

Everything's going to be okay. I am here now.

"I feel it," I whisper.

Yes, you feel it.

Maybe you don't understand what any of this means. Quiet. This is peaceful. You're going to forget about everything that doesn't matter.

Things aren't so cold anymore. The night is still. Out across the valley, the sky is dark but the streetlights glow like small fires. There are no more battles in the silence. Hush and wane. The candles are blown out. The music is turned off. A layer of ego has been peeled away.

Feel the coolness.

Feel the way the storm moves through and out your body. Hear the way we say the things that aren't there.

There's a wild buffalo spirit inside you.

CHAPTER 30

I got back to my site on November 2. Around then I started working with the Department of Environment at the municipality. This came after an aborted attempt to work with Raúl, the womanizing former mayor. When everyone at FODI was fired, Winkler suggested that I help Raúl with his new foundation, which had some sort of environmental theme to it. My work with Raúl lasted exactly two meetings. In the first, he invited me to an "important session" he "needed me for" on a Saturday. I sat and listened as he talked to a group of tilapia farmers for over three hours; my only contribution was when he told me to go downstairs and across the street to fetch everyone some water.

The other meeting took place at his house between the two of us. During the conversation, he winked at me as he admitted he was using the foundation to launder grant money he received through his brother who worked in the provincial government.

When I decided things weren't going anywhere with Raúl, I went into the municipality and introduced myself to the new mayor and told him why I was there. He brought me to the environmental department's head, a small round man with thick glasses named Benito, who then introduced me to the rest of the department.

Benito told me I could help them with a watershed project near Zumbi. They were planning to clean up one of the river systems that started up in the hills to the east and fed down to Zumbi and the Rio

Zamora. The project included working with the communities along the river to plant trees and build fences to help reduce the pollution runoff. When I told Winkler about it over the phone, he practically squealed with joy.

After many days and weeks of being told to come back tomorrow, I finally went with two engineers from the Department of Environment to the community where they wanted to start the watershed project. We hitched a ride in a dump truck and wound up the tiny dirt roads for forty-five minutes. I didn't do much talking at the meeting other than to introduce myself as a Peace Corps volunteer and say that I'd be assisting with this project. About fifty people from the community arrived and crammed into one room of the local schoolhouse.

The municipal workers explained the project and invited audience members to talk about goods and services their community lacked. People raised their hands to cite everything from a soccer field to a health clinic.

Then a man with one ear filibustered for the rest of the meeting. Standing at the back of the room, he talked without pausing or really even making a point. People started to leave. He went on for another half an hour and the meeting ended with a whimper. The municipal workers and I hitched a ride back to Zumbi.

MIDWAY THROUGH NOVEMBER, WINKLER CAME down to visit my site. We met with Benito and he told Winkler all about the watershed project. Afterward, Winkler seemed happy. He told me he thought Peace Corps volunteers who worked in offices every day were the only ones who mattered.

A week later, I went back to the municipality and found out Benito was no longer working there. The watershed project had been canceled, someone told me. I turned around and walked home.

I n those days I walked the streets feeling like a shell of a human. The sweltering, dusty streets were chipping away at my soul, little by little. I woke up every morning glued to the mattress—unable to wake up at a reasonable hour and too lethargic to roll out of bed. Sometimes I embraced the loneliness, like somehow it was making me tougher or, in more masochistic moments, like it was making me stronger because the lonelier you are the more you know what dying feels like. But mostly it was just dull, hot loneliness. I was too tired to do anything and too depressed to even jerk off (a phenomenon I'd only experienced once or twice before in my life). My lungs were full of lead.

I thought I was losing my mind—literally. I'd be walking around or eating or—worse—just lying there *thinking* and my mind would start racing so fast that I wasn't sure I could ever get it to slow down again. And this was happening more and more every day.

One night, too tired to cook, I walked a hundred yards down to one of the roadside restaurants and ordered another plate of tasteless carbohydrates. I looked at the table and it didn't feel right. I looked at the people around me, and their shiny faces were smacking on food and talking but I couldn't hear the sounds. I looked at my hands and they trembled. My heart now pumped so hard I was afraid it would tire out and stop, leaving me on the floor dying while other patrons assumed I was another drunk just taking his time crawling out the door. And this time my mind really raced until I thought I'd spend the rest of my sad life muttering incoherently to myself, unable to keep pace with the million racing thoughts.

I stood up to go to the sink in the corner and splash water over my face. I ended up getting my whole head wet. I returned to my table, where I sat down and realized I couldn't breathe. I looked down at the food and up at the wall—I thought there was something significant about that spot on the wall: fading yellow paint to the left of the TV that blared home video–quality *telenovelas* while the other eaters chomped away at chicken bones with their bare hands and mouths wide open. The spot on the wall led to another million thoughts at once. Now my heart really wanted to lurch out of my chest and onto the plate in front of me.

I got up from my untouched chicken and rice and made it out to the street where I felt like I could finally take full breaths. I turned the corner and made it down to the dark abandoned streets away from the center of town. I looked side to side and up at the blank sky to make sure I was alone. No one was near me. Finally, I felt my heart winding down like a giant machine being shut off after revving at full throttle. The beats were slower but each hit hard like a big drum. My mind came back down from above and reentered my skull. I thought I'd be all right. I decided people were the problem.

Thus began a period of instability in which I was sure that being in the presence of more than one person at a time would cripple my ability to function on any level. I feared getting on buses because if I had another attack of anxiety, I'd have nowhere to go. If I did leave the relative comfort of my bedroom, I'd view any group of people as a gang of bloodthirsty killers. I was too tired to talk to anyone. I was too angry and upset to spend much time outside my room. My nuts and prostate were once again flaring up regularly into debilitating and gut-clenching lightning bolts of pain.

After a couple more weeks of this, I called the Peace Corps medical office. The person I actually spoke with was a temporary doctor from another Peace Corps country who was filling in while our doctors were in D.C. for a conference. I told her all about it. She told me the usual doctors would be in contact with me when they got back in town.

I never heard from anyone.

ON DECEMBER 1, AFTER FIVE months with Graciela and Consuela and a total of nine months living with Ecuadorian host families, I was finally able to move into my own place. I'd found a bungalow apartment just off the square in the center of the town. On one of my last days at the house, I said hello, as usual, to Consuela's handicapped sister, who'd never acknowledged me and usually stared at the ground whenever I passed. But this time, out of the blue, she looked up, stared me right in the eyes, and said with a lucid smile, "*Buenos días, ¿cómo estás?*" I stared back in disbelief because first, I was too shocked to even respond, and second, it was exactly like the scene out of *One Flew over the Cuckoo's Nest* when the big Indian who everyone thought was mute all of a sudden says thank you to the Jack Nicholson character, who of course can't believe his ears. The next time I saw Consuela's sister, I said hello again and she went back to ignoring me and scavenging for rocks in the yard.

Consuela's kids—especially her youngest, whom I got along with—were sad to see me go. Consuela told me, with a wink, to make sure I stopped by and visited as much as I could. I took four trips carrying my belongings three blocks to the other side of town and came back for the last time to drop off my old set of keys. Graciela waddled out into the yard and snarled, "Did you leave the sheets?"

"Yes, I washed and dried them—they're on the mattress," I said.

I thanked her for sharing her house with me these last months. I told her to take care and enjoy the holidays. She stood there silently and stuck out her hand for the keys.

CHAPTER 32

Christmas was coming. And it was close to a full year since I'd seen my brother. He was midway through his final year of law school, and four months before, he bought tickets to come visit over the New Year. We planned to spend a couple of days at my site—more than enough time for him to get the gist of how I lived—then fly to Cartagena, Colombia, for a week on the beach with another friend of ours. I was looking forward to showing him what my life here was like, but I was much more eager for Colombia, which would finally be a vacation for the both of us.

As if it weren't depressing enough being alone and far from family on Christmas, the sights and sounds in Zumbi didn't make it easier. Despite being highly Catholic, the Ecuadorians didn't think much of Christmas. Fair enough. After all, the American brand of Christmas is not really a religious one. There was something about the alternating heat and downpours and the few weak attempts at decorations—a fake tree lit up here, some pathetic tinsel there—that made this extra depressing.

One day, Steven, the twelve-year-old who lived across a courtyard from my new apartment, asked if Santa was real.

"Of course," I said.

"And he makes all the toys on Christmas?" he asked.

"Well, actually he has a bunch of little helper people," I said, a direct translation for "elves" not coming to mind, "and he just delivers the toys on Christmas Eve."

Steven nodded as if it made perfect sense. "And he goes to all the homes where you're from?"

I nodded.

"Then why doesn't he come to Ecuador?" he asked.

"Well, sure he does, he goes everywhere," I assured him.

His mother walked out their front door to chime in. "No, he's never come here," she said matter-of-factly. She wanted to know why. I assumed she was playing along, just like me.

"Well, maybe it's because he doesn't speak Spanish," I said.

The look in Steven's eyes told me that this made perfect sense. But the look in his mother's eyes revealed the mistake I'd made. She, too, thought that Santa Claus really delivered toys to Americans on Christmas. This thirty-two-year-old mother and her young son couldn't understand why Ecuador wasn't as lucky to be graced by his jolly presence. I'd flippantly given them an answer to a major question in their lives.

Over the following year, as Steven became a teenager, I attempted to compensate for this conversation by giving some straight talk whenever I got the opportunity. When he asked if Superman and Spiderman were real and living in the States, I said no. He responded by informing me that I was full of shit and of course they existed.

MY BROTHER, ANDREW, WAS FLYING into Guayaquil on the twenty-seventh. I decided it would be too disheartening to actually stay at my site on Christmas day, so I got on a bus for several hours and headed to a hostel in Vilcabamba where I could hang out with some backpackers who also found themselves far from home on Christmas. Vilcabamba is one of Ecuador's few non-beach, non-Galápagos destinations that tourists pass through with any sort of regularity (and even then, due to the fact that it's fourteen hours south of Quito, ten hours from Guayaquil, and six hours from Cuenca, it's not exactly a hot spot of tourism). I figured that I'd find at least some English speakers to talk to. On Christmas Eve day, I got on a 5 a.m. bus out of my site.

The weather in Vilcabamba is nearly always perfect: mild, dry, and sunny. This time it was no different. I relaxed by the pool and met the travelers there. The group was your typical cross-section of globetrotters you'd find anywhere: some Canadians and Australians, a couple of Brits, and some Europeans—usually German or French. They were all friendly.

I had plenty of opportunities for the same conversation I had every time I ran into other foreigners: I ask them how long they've been passing through these parts. They give me a rundown of their journey and time in South America. "And what about you?" they ask. "Oh, I live here," I say. Sometimes, depending on where I am, I'll point my finger, "About a five-hour bus trip in that direction." Then comes the scripted conversation about my Peace Corps experience. And what an experience it must be! Sometimes they'll ooh and ahh and comment on how difficult that time and distance away probably is. Even the ones who aren't interested do a magnificent job of pretending. The Americans have all heard of the Peace Corps and most of the foreigners have, too; most are legitimately interested in what my life here is like and why I chose to do it.

At the hostel, I was having this conversation by the pool with an Australian man my age. He was a hulking sort of guy—the type I imagined being in a brutal Australian surfer gang. After I described what I did and what it was all about, he said loud enough for the others lounging around the pool to hear, "That's really something! There's U.S. power at work, doing good around the world. You only ever hear bad things about them yanks—fighting everybody's wars, being arrogant—but look at this guy here. Ha! That's incredible!"

His passion embarrassed me a little. There was a Canadian couple nearby and I could feel them rolling their eyes. I'm not sure if it was because of the Australian's monologue or because of his manner itself. He was loud, bordering on obnoxious. But I liked talking with him. We talked some more that afternoon. It reminded me how the reputation that Americans have gotten overseas for being loud, rude, and disrespectful—being the "ugly American"—was wrong or at least outdated. In my experience, if anyone has filled that role, it's the Brits or the Aussies. Perhaps in backlash to knowing this stereotype haunts us, most traveling Americans I see try hard to be reserved, polite, and hyper-aware of local customs. I suppose there are many who would prove me wrong, but then that's the problem with stereotypes.

As the sun went down, everyone ate and then migrated to the bar.

I also met an Australian woman my age who'd been traveling alone in South America for a few months. She was skinny but gorgeous, with curly auburn hair, fair skin, and dark eyes. We drank liquor all night and talked about South America. Somewhere between whisky shots, the clock struck midnight and it was Christmas. With my head spinning, I went to bed in my cabin and she in hers. I remember just wanting to lie down next to her and smell her hair. That would have been nice.

I woke up on Christmas day and got on the Internet while eating breakfast in the hostel's dining area. I sent an email I'd prewritten to a doctor back home—the father of a fellow volunteer I'd contacted before about my medical difficulties. He said he would try to connect me with a "team of urologists" he worked with in the U.S. The email began with the usual greetings, then continued with a rundown on the entire history of my illness—from the first electric jolt of pain in my testicles to the trials I'd gone through since then, complete with throbbing nuts, an aching prostate, and a rectal sonogram. My hope was that I would have some answers after the New Year. If not, that one-year-in-country mark in February was looking better and better as a time to throw in the towel and take my aching man parts back home with an excuse to leave that no one could ever blame me for.

While online, I read news websites for the Christmassy stuff and for an update on the world. Most of it focused on the fact that we were getting ready to say goodbye (or, more appropriately, good riddance) to another decade. Everyone was coming out with their top-ten lists for this or that—movies, sports events, political goings-on. It seemed to me it couldn't have been a worse decade. The "zeroes" or "aughts" essentially began with the September 11 attacks, and then descended into wars, a worsening environment, and, to cap things off, a financial disaster that sent ripples around the world. During this time, we of course got iPods and HDTV, but no solutions to any of the things that mattered. In all, it was a decade so disastrous, it's probably fitting we could never even agree on what to call it.

The one glimmer of hope before I left for Ecuador was the election of Obama (like him or not, his election did say something about our country), but lately even that was beginning to feel like a giant letdown. I wasn't the only person struggling to see what had actually changed about the way we did government.

Using the fast Internet to catch up on the news wasn't necessarily a good idea.

I got away from the computer and went to the pool. I drank rum and smoked Honduran cigars with a guy from Detroit who'd been traveling everywhere south of the United States for the last six months. He was in his thirties and had saved up for almost ten years so he could drop everything and backpack around Latin America. He said he was spending about twenty dollars a day and could afford to go on for another six months.

That night was more low-key than the previous. I beat a German guy in the championship match of a ping-pong tournament and won a fifth of rum to take home with me. I went to bed early and left the next morning as the sun was coming up. I planned to take the bus back to Zumbi and prepare for my brother's visit before turning around the next day and heading for Loja, where I'd catch a plane to Guayaquil to greet Andrew when he landed.

CHAPTER 33

The prop plane I boarded for Guayaquil had room for eighteen passengers. As we ascended out of the valley west of Loja, I saw a beautiful patchwork of sugarcane fields cradled by the dry landscape. The plane immediately banked up to get over the high mountains surrounding the valley, and seconds later, we were in the clouds.

The trip from Loja to Guayaquil is ten hours by bus, but forty minutes by plane. We landed in the late afternoon, and I killed several hours at the airport until my brother arrived. Seeing a member of my family for the first time in nearly a year was almost too good to be true. We hugged and then hustled to find a taxi.

We planned to sleep a few hours at a nearby hotel since we had an early flight back to Loja the following morning. At the time, I didn't want to spend a minute more than we had to in Guayaquil.

I never liked the city in the first place—big and dirty and filled with people who reminded me too much of my neighbors in La Segua. But also, we'd been receiving crime updates by email lately and many of them occurred in Guayaquil. In addition to emails from Pilar about Peace Corps–related incidents and warnings, we'd gotten several from the Regional Security Officers with the U.S. Embassy. The crimes were increasingly gruesome—and more and more of them were involving the same express kidnappings that the volunteer described to us during training.

A recent case concerned two American couples and was like most other express kidnappings, except that at the end, the two wives were raped before being dropped off with their husbands in the middle of nowhere. Reading that email turned my stomach. It made me even more cynical about Ecuador's hopes of tourism becoming the life-blood of its economy. *Who's going to come here if you can't safely use a taxi in the country's richest city?* I thought.

This was all circling through my head, but fortunately my brother and I were together in that city for less than seven hours.

Andrew came bearing gifts of magazines, flavored sunflower seeds, and a new pair of shoes. I barely slept and the next morning we were up and out of there. Andrew took one look at the plane (the very one I'd taken the evening before) and shook his head laughing, "You sure about this?" We both smiled and talked about the thrills of the developing world.

The plane ride was quick and easy. Then we hopped on a bus for the four-hour ride to Zumbi.

I'd taken the bus between my site and Loja so many times, I'd almost forgotten that the twists and turns down shoddy roads at lu-natic speeds could be startling for a newcomer. Andrew took it in stride, often shaking his head in disbelief. I, for whatever reason, felt the urge to let out my frustrations with the various nuisances. At one point, we were stopped for half an hour while a beer truck that had just crashed was cleared off the road. Shattered bottles were littered everywhere. Foamy beer washed across the pavement.

"How does someone manage to get into an accident like that?" my brother asked.

"Easy," I said. "Ecuadorians were driving, that's how." And it all came pouring out like this probably because I normally had no one to share these everyday absurdities with.

Though he was older, I couldn't help feeling like I was looking after my brother while he was there. First off, he spoke no Spanish. So I fretted about translating everything. And I stressed about making sure our trip went smoothly and making him feel comfortable and not letting things fall apart on his one and only visit to my alternate universe. I got all worked up feeling the responsibility.

When our bus stopped at Zamora, midway between Loja and Zumbi, Andrew hopped out to run to the bathroom. I gave him the nickel it would cost to use the facilities and I told him to hurry. For a country with a flimsy relationship with time, bus terminals were the one place that had little margin for error. I knew the bus would pull back out of the station in just a minute or two.

When the gears shifted into reverse a minute later and Andrew still wasn't back, I stood up, my fists clenched into white knuckles, looking to see if he was on his way back. I began sweating. I didn't see him, but the bus hadn't begun to pull all the way out just yet. Right when I was about to yell at the driver to stop and wait, I saw my brother walking up nonchalantly, as if there were time to spare. I felt like yelling at him, "What the fuck! You can't dillydally around like that, you gotta hurry, man. Don't do that to me again!" But I managed to hold it in.

"Wow, he was getting ready to leave," Andrew said. "Did I make you nervous?"

"Yeah," I said, shrugging it off with a chuckle.

My paranoia and protectiveness carried on when we got to my site. I'd only been in the apartment a month. It was scant for furniture: In the main room, just a desk, a table, and some plastic chairs; in my bedroom, just a crappy mattress on a bed frame it didn't fit and a splintery dresser I piled my clothes into. For now at least, it was the bare bones. And when we walked in, the apartment stank: While I was gone, a rat had eaten the poison under my sink and crawled inside the wall to die.

I wanted my brother to get an impression of how I lived. But with him finally there, I was embarrassed. When I saw him walk out the front door to my outside bathroom wrapped in a towel and wearing my ragged sandals to take a shower, or hunch over at the too-low sink with the garden-hose-looking faucet in my kitchen, or struggle with the smell of the dead rat that was decomposing in an unreachable space in my wall, or trip across the shredded linoleum on my floor, or look at my foam twin-size mattress with a sinkhole in the middle, I was reminded of where I lived. It pissed me off. All I could hope was that the cats didn't choose that week to unleash another volley of piss down from the rafters. (When I told my new landlady about the cats pissing through my ceiling, her response was, "There are no cats here.")

Andrew offered to buy me a nicer chair. He couldn't stand to see me sitting at my desk in the ass-numbing plastic patio chair I'd bought for six bucks.

"No!" I said. "I don't need a new goddamn chair." I felt lonely just saying this out loud. Perhaps it was the ego factor of feeling like I needed to rough it, but I sure as hell wasn't in the mood for anyone's help—and certainly not their pity.

"What's your problem? I was just offering to help," he said with a scowl that made me feel worthless. "It'd be my gift to you."

"It's because I feel like with every comment it seems you're reminding me of what a shit hole I live in. Whether it's the chairs or the crappy linoleum floor or the shit food, or the way Zumbi moves in slow motion . . ."

He shook his head and we were quiet for a while and let it drop.

Zumbi was, indeed, moving in slow motion—even more so than usual. The heat was so heavy and strong that stepping outside into the white glare didn't feel anything like the damp Amazon that my brother was expecting. I showed him everything there was to see rather quickly, and not surprisingly, there wasn't much else to do. One afternoon, we went to the derelict soccer field at the local high school and tossed my football around. I'd brought the ball with me from home a year earlier and this was the first time I'd inflated it. The next day we went on a hike and got a good view looking down on Zumbi from up in the foothills. We turned around to head back when we both felt like we were getting heat sickness.

For a spare mattress, I'd borrowed a two-inch-thick roll-up thing from a neighbor and put it on my floor with a sleeping bag. My brother was so uncomfortable the first night that I offered to take it the next two. My bed wasn't a huge upgrade or anything—especially since I had only one sheet at the time—but he seemed pleased.

Several months later, I would grow comfortable in that little apartment, once I had time to make it mine. After those few days with my brother, though, I was happy to leave it—and Zumbi. Our last night there, we both lay in our beds talking late into the night. He couldn't go to sleep and my balls were flaring up. I talked a little bit about how much pain I was in and how I'd thought about Early Terminating because at least at home I could sit in pain with some relative comfort around me.

I wanted to say so much but couldn't get it out. I didn't know where to start. I felt disconnected from everyone and everything. It was suffocating. But I kept it to myself and we spent the late hours talking about all the places we'd traveled to together and how, by far, this felt the strangest. We talked about that and whatever else came to our minds that didn't cause too much laboring to get out in the open.

I was relieved to lock the door behind me and head out on my first real vacation in a year. Andrew pointed out that this was probably the first time in history that anyone had been relieved to go *into* Colombia because it meant they finally could, as I'd said, *let their guard down.*

PART THREE

The Electric Love

CHAPTER 34

I returned from vacation to an email about my balls and prostate. The doctor I'd been in touch with in the States had heard back from his team of urologists. They'd all weighed in and agreed on the epididymitis-prostatitis diagnosis and recommended a continued regimen of tepid-water scrotum soaking.

While noting that even stress could be causing my symptoms, the lead urologist seemed almost sure that I'd come across a tricky strain of E. coli. In a sentence that made my heart sink, he pointed out that symptoms like mine could last up to two or three years.

He recommended more Cipro and said I should try staying away from spicy foods and vitamin C—anything that was increasing the acidity in my urine. Also, it appeared that pain relievers, which I'd been popping like Pez since that first day the throbbing and piercing set in, were a part of the problem, not the solution. I was a little nervous about more Cipro, since I'd already taken the powerful antibiotic for nearly the entire month of November, but I was willing to give anything one last try to reduce the pain.

So I unleashed a pharmaceutical blitzkrieg that left me dizzy, cranky, and easily sunburned. Over the next several weeks, the pain went from frequent cattle prod-like bolts to occasional piercing sensations.

❖ ❖ ❖

WHEN A WOMAN IN ZUMBI—TO whom I'd described the purpose of the Peace Corps several times—asked me if I was there on vacation, I knew I needed to find a real project. I'd used the municipal firings and my man plumbing as excuses long enough. The only thing I had done to stay busy the previous two months was teach English to two women from the municipality. It was a task I promised myself I'd never stoop to, because I believed that the Peace Corps was about *real* development work—but I was bored.

My English lessons usually degenerated into my students telling me—in Spanish—all the town's juicy gossip, which was enthralling. Once we even plunged into the depths of anthropology: They reluctantly admitted they had some indigenous blood in them but became enraged when I said I was fairly positive I didn't have any North American Indian blood in me. Hashing out the differences wasn't easy.

As for actually learning English, my students became dissatisfied with my inability to teach them through osmosis. Frustrated that they weren't yet fluent in "gringo speak" after a week or two, they lost interest and the lessons quickly fizzled out.

It was a new year. I'd been living in Zumbi seven months. It had been about five months since the women at FODI had left. And although the pain in my balls and prostate was still there, it was no longer quite the debilitating lightning strikes through my man plumbing that made me double over on the sidewalk. I could finally get outdoors and function. I decided it was time to get something to *do.*

One morning I got out of the shower and walked back around to the front door of my apartment, where two men in dress shirts stood knocking. They were the principal and vice principal from Zumbi's only high school.

Carlito, the principal, did all the talking. He reminded me of a modern version of the *caudillos* who ruled South American hamlets with an iron fist in the days of yore. Short and barrel-chested, he almost always had a cigarette dangling from his lips beneath his long gray mustache. Most noticeably, he was missing one of his front teeth. He had a demeanor that would have scared the shit out of me had I been one of his students. But since I was viewed as some sort of authority figure—or more likely, someone with access to money—it would always seem like he was kissing up to me. He constantly smiled, offered me cigarettes, and, later on, would clear people out of his office every time I came to see him, referring to me as his "esteemed colleague."

In a lengthy preamble, Carlito explained that the facilities of the high school were simply not up to snuff. (Indeed, the one time I'd gone there to check the place out, the classrooms appeared as though they'd been abandoned. Other than the shoddy desks, there were no materials to be found. And in place of actual chalkboards was a section of the wall painted green. The most elaborate classroom was the science lab, which was equally as drab, but had both a dog skeleton and a jar with a human fetus.)

The long and short of it was that Carlito wanted to build a greenhouse, but not just any greenhouse—a greenhouse that would be the envy of all other academic institutions in the area. The high school had a huge amount of property—several acres of farmland that the military gave to them years back—but none of it was being put to good use. Up until then, they were simply renting out tracts to people for grazing their cows.

To go hand in hand with the project, Carlito wanted to revamp the school's outdoor science curriculum. Even though we were in a section of the world that was a natural greenhouse—where you could drop any type of seed and it would grow—the greenhouse was a good idea. Because it rained so hard, many crops actually needed cover. But most important, it would be the epicenter of an outdoor classroom where students could do hands-on environmental education work every day.

I said yes to Carlito. Of course I wanted to do this. If he'd told me they wanted to tear down some classrooms and put in a swimming pool, I probably would have said yes just to get off my ass and start working.

The next day, I began searching for the different funding channels available to volunteers. The most straightforward method was a grant set up through the U.S. Department of Agriculture. Someone in the Peace Corps office once described to me that this money came from a pool of cash from leftover farm subsidies. I always thought this was a bittersweet irony—that the overflow from the very subsidies that made it impossible for farmers in developing countries like this one to compete were filtered back to them in the form of four-figure grants, administered by twenty-four-year-old volunteers.

So I embarked on a several-month process that I referred to as the twenty-first-century Peace Corps experience: living on my own way out in the jungle, yet being bogged down with . . . paperwork. In a twenty-page grant proposal, I laid out the parameters of the project: the idea, the costs, the construction company, the timetable, the tasks and people involved, and the ways it was sustainable. If I had been doing this on my own, it would have taken about a week, but since the local government was involved, it would be about five months before I sent in the final draft to the Peace Corps office.

The grant required that 25 percent of the total project cost be provided by local project partners. Therefore, on top of the $7,000 I could get from the grant, we needed about $2,300 more to reach that 25 percent. For us, this meant going to the mayor and asking for money to go toward the cost of the materials and construction. Some came in the form of cash, which the mayor agreed to, and the rest was in the form of in-kind contributions, like soil and tractor use. This in-kind portion meant that eventually my accounting, while technically accurate, would be what you might call *creative*.

At one point during the process, it took me about three months to get the municipal government to print out a signed piece of paper agreeing to pay their portion of the costs. When I finally got the thing, it was a glorious and formidable example of third-world bureaucracy—so overly official and faux professional that it was somewhat charming. The document had about five notarized stamps from various departments and so many vast swirling signatures that even someone in the Peace Corps office deemed it "impressive."

It became increasingly obvious that the more Ecuadorians were involved, the harder and more needlessly complicated things became. This was a fact I never felt bad about thinking, given that the Peace Corps continually warned us about it throughout training, using nearly the same phrasing.

THE NEXT FEW MONTHS CONSISTED of me typing up documents on my laptop inside my apartment and occasionally walking across town to the municipal building to ask a small favor, which would normally take a week or two to reconcile. (During this time, I also founded and served as editor of a quarterly newsmagazine for Peace Corps Ecuador, which kept me busy and in front of the computer for a few hours every day.)

All the sitting at my desk didn't do much to convince my neighbors that I was doing anything for their community, but the grant gave me the peace of mind that I had a "project" going. Plus, now when Winkler called me or sent ominous messages and emails, I could ramble on about how I was working on The Grant Project and how things were *this close* to coming together.

He and I had been at an awkward impasse for several months, which consisted of him giving me shit for not having any project partners, but being passive-aggressive about it, since he knew it was mostly his fault that I was out there idling, without a counterpart. All the while, I didn't feel comfortable telling him that the reason I hadn't been moving mountains in my community was because my balls hurt me too much to stand up and all the Cipro was making me delirious.

CHAPTER 35

Over Easter weekend I traveled to a jungle town about eleven hours north to visit a volunteer who wanted to have sex. She'd been nudging me into visiting her for many months, ever since I declined her invitation to meet for a night at a random place halfway between our two sites. Her calls and texts urging me to come were nothing if not aggressive and uncharming. But I hadn't had sex in a very long time. So I went.

When the new country director arrived in November, he instituted a new Out of Site Policy. Among other changes, it was renamed the Whereabouts Policy. Before, we were able to go anywhere in the country as long as we were back at our site within seventy-two hours. Now the seventy-two-hour restriction was gone, but we were limited to traveling within an imaginary radius of roughly five hours away from our sites. This meant relatively little to me, already being so isolated from everything and everyone else in the country, but some volunteers took this, and other changes, pretty seriously and wrote nasty letters to the office, sometimes cc'ing all 150 other volunteers on their emails. They were the types of letters that included sentences beginning with: "It is imperative that . . ."

In any event, this meant that for my trip up north I had to ask for special permission. I was allowed to go only because it was the holiday weekend. But as a result of submitting my proposed itinerary, Winkler had a pretty good idea that I was traveling a half day for some sex and knew the exact woman that sex was going to involve.

The bus ride through the southern part of Ecuador's Amazon is probably the most pleasing road trip you can take in the country. Going an average of twenty-five miles an hour the entire time, you get to look off to the east and see nothing but jungle. Each town you pass through feels like the final frontier. And when it gets completely dark, you can press your cheek up against the cool glass of the window and see nothing but the stars overhead and a few oil platforms blinking out across the Amazon.

I arrived in the volunteer's town at 1 a.m. on Friday and she met me at the bus station looking drowsy.

As we lay in her bed after our first go at it, she turned to me and said, "I haven't had sex in like a year. What about you?"

"I don't know," I said.

Her long curly hair spread out over the pillow. I was thinking about how strange it all was.

"What's the longest you've ever gone without sex before?" she said.

"Eighteen years."

For the rest of the weekend we cooked and laughed and listened to music and had a good time. But I wasn't in the mood for any more sex. Part of it was her, and part of it was the shame of feeling as though we were like animals who couldn't go without it. But I joylessly had sex a few more times before the weekend was over, including once when she'd talked me into using a sex toy she kept in the drawer of her nightstand.

Afterward, I didn't even want to think about sex for a long time. As I lay there, I told her I planned on taking the six o'clock bus back to my site the next morning. She let out a disapproving groan and said I should get on a later bus so I could fuck her once more before I left. I mumbled something about how my leaving at six and fucking her one last time weren't mutually exclusive. She persisted on and we went to sleep. At 5:25 I awoke to her pivoting herself atop me. And I was reminded then that there are few things lonelier in life than sex with someone you don't care for.

As the sun rose over the jungle fog, I began the long ride south to my site, winding up and down dirt roads through the green hills, stopping only to buy snacks and use the bathroom at filthy roadside diners. It was Easter morning in the Amazon.

I saw large, morose-looking religious processions in the streets. Pigs getting roasted with blowtorches on the side of the road. Children selling fried chicken and boiled yucca at the bus stops.

I saw papaya groves and acres of deforestation with cows grazing. Roadside shrines to the Virgin Mary surrounded by fresh flowers and Christmas lights.

I saw women bent down doing laundry in stream beds. Shirtless drunks asleep on sidewalks or park benches or facedown in gutters. Other men with two or more missing limbs hoisting themselves into the bus to wobble up and down the aisle asking for spare change.

I saw beautiful indigenous girls listening to bad music on their cell phones. Black people selling coconut milk. Kids playing soccer. Women burning trash. Teens wearing WWF shirts and Yankees hats. And men peeing in the road.

I saw ducks and chickens pecking at the Styrofoam trash that had been flung from bus windows onto the damp ground.

And I saw moms with babies—lots of babies.

I knew that I would look back and feel connected to this jungle and maybe sorta kinda miss it. I saw all the frontier towns and wondered what it was like living there—was it just like Zumbi? Or was it lonelier, or not as boring, or filled with all the same characters who every day kept me laughing and smiling and cursing? I listened to music on my iPod and then sometimes just looked out the window in silence thinking about how naïve it was to imagine I could come down here and wake up one day knowing exactly what I wanted to do with the rest of my life.

I thought about how, all things considered, it had been nice to finally hold someone in my arms (and I thought about how just having a thought like that was a sign I'd been isolated for a long time). With the window cracked and music playing and my backpack in my lap and nothing but bumpy open road ahead, I wished bus rides like this would never end.

ometime around then I'm in Loja for a weekend and I meet a girl. And then I'm in Loja a lot more. Out dancing. Going to dinner. Walking on the narrow sidewalks arm in arm. Getting ice cream in her parents' café. Drinking together in dark bars on weeknights with live music while she smokes cigarettes and leans in for kisses. It goes on like this for several weeks.

She is twenty-five years old and beautiful. Born and raised in Loja, she has traveled to the States and Europe and speaks English. And we always see each other in Loja—never at my site. She is the type of upper-class Lojana who would prefer to pretend that places like Zumbi don't exist. If I ever brought her to my site, it's unclear what exactly would disgust her the most, but she would surely unload an entire bottle of Purell by the time we reached my doorstep.

But she's beautiful and sexy. She's so beautiful that other guys are always staring at her when we walk into restaurants and bars. And she acts like she doesn't know why. She's so beautiful I dig into my U.S. bank account for late lunches on the weekends after nights when we've stayed out late drinking and the next day our clothes still smell like whisky and stale smoke. (She does *not* settle for pathetic two-dollar lunches with the commoners.) She's so beautiful I tolerate her smoking and even look at the way the plumes of smoke leave her lips and disappear above us in the dim lights of the nightclubs and think it's . . . sexy.

One day we're in one of those nice restaurants with the white tablecloths and the other Lojanos in their very expensive but ill-fitting suits. We're on the far end of town past the old church and on the way to the stadium. I'm tired. I look at the menu and it all looks expensive and unappetizing to me but I order the ceviche, which turns out to be awful and later that day I will take a lonely bus ride over the mountain pass and down into the Amazon on a empty stomach and twenty-five dollars poorer. It's a clear and warm Sunday.

I've been seeing her a few weeks now so I feel comfortable telling her about my epididymal/prostatic infection and the ensuing pain that lasted six months and necessitated trips to Loja and Quito and—yes—multiple testicular sonograms. She listens with vague amusement. I also tell her about how I got pickpocketed but how it wasn't a big deal because I only had like two bucks in my wallet and all the other important stuff was squirreled away in my shoes and other pockets and how I really just missed the wallet.

She laughs, but it's not a ha-ha laugh; it's a pity laugh. She smiles and leans over and kisses me and pours herself another lemonade and barks something else at the waiter and then stares me in the eye and says, "Why are you still in this country?"

WEEKS LATER WE SIT IN her parents' living room eating big slices of mango for breakfast. I've just come back from another administrative trip to Quito and I'm stopping in Loja for the night before returning to Zumbi. Hanging on the wall in front of me is a giant painting of Jesus wearing a crown of thorns. The painting is so vivid and grotesque it looks as if the blood from his forehead could drip right off the wall and down onto the Persian rug.

Today is the day it ends and we can't be seeing each other anymore and I tell her this. She is surprised when I tell her, which is strange since just a week earlier she told me she had a boyfriend and in a few months would be moving to Belgium to work as an au pair and be with him, which is especially strange since he lives in Holland. She just *has to* get out of this country that she loves so much but can't stand to live in. She wants to go to the U.S. again if she can, but keeps getting denied a visa. (It turns out that the last time she was there, she worked while on a student visa, which means she'll likely never be allowed to return—a piece of news I broke to her gently.) But this is all just a side note. She's leaving soon for Europe and for some European man she's been talking to on the phone every day this whole time and she's *surprised* that I'm walking away from it all.

All of this makes my mind race. It races through why I can't manage any long relationships and then it races through all the circumstances (there are always circumstances) and from there it races through all the reasons and I wonder if her (or any woman) not understanding me is still a valid reason for breaking up. (The year before, I'd broken up with another volunteer I'd dated very briefly and when I told her that I couldn't "do this anymore," she said, "You're leaving the Peace Corps?" I paused and continued, "Well, no . . .")

Right now, here on the couch, I think about all this and I feel sick to my stomach. It's a throbbing aching feeling of sickness that I can't shake. (I find out a week later that this is not the result of acute heartache but a combination of amoebas, E. coli, and worms—a triple play of intestinal issues.) She leans toward me and I'm not sure if she wants to kiss me or tackle me. I just look up at the painting of Jesus, who stares back down at me. Suddenly her cigarette smoking isn't sexy anymore. All I can think is I should have ended this weeks ago on that Sunday when I ordered the bad ceviche.

CHAPTER 37

In May I received an invitation from the Peace Corps asking for my "mandatory attendance" at a Resiliency Workshop the following month in the central sierra city of Cuenca. Most of the volunteers from the southern half of the country would be there. The "invitation" didn't say what kinds of topics would be covered, but they turned out to focus mostly on *hanging in there*. This was odd because I was always under the impression that the Peace Corps did its best to weed out the lightweights during the application process, not coddle them once they were at their sites. Even stranger, roughly half the volunteers at the workshop were completing their service in just two months. But I couldn't complain about a free trip to Cuenca.

We enjoyed our three days and two nights in what is probably Ecuador's cleanest and most beautiful city. The daytime activities harkened back to my training exactly a year earlier: We sat together in a room and withstood a battery of group sessions and activities and evaluations. One activity was a card game designed to show us how we made decisions. A language segment to the workshop required that we go out on a scavenger hunt through the city. We talked about taking risks; we talked about things that are difficult; we talked about the definition of stress.

And we heard happy stories. Volunteers who were about to complete their two years and hadn't gotten much done but had forged relationships that they'd cherish forever. Or volunteers for whom the stars had aligned who ended up at sites where gung-ho counterparts helped them form wildly successful beekeeping operations or fertilizer factories.

Then, in another session, I found out that there is a legitimate term for what I, and pretty much everyone else there, had been experiencing at certain points during my time in country: compassion fatigue. Apparently, this term gets tossed around in the expatriate/ development world to describe what happens when people get fed up with the work they're doing and the people they're doing it for. Due to the stress or frustration or despair from having things go wrong or working with host country nationals who don't care, the pendulum shifts from having empathy for these people to feeling unsympathetic or even hostile toward them. This is a component of the larger issue of culture shock. Of course, whenever we got to talking about that, there were always great stories to be had, such as the one about a guy who got in a cab with some other volunteers and, upon learning that the cab driver planned on charging him $1.50 instead of $1.00 to travel across town, lurched forward in his seat screaming, "Oh fuck you!"

Lastly, we received a refresher safety and security session on, among other things, what to do in the event of coastal flooding—a curious exercise given that everyone at the conference lived either in the Amazon or in the sierra, at several thousand feet of elevation. Other notable highlights from the conference: One volunteer got up to ask a question and said "fuck" about five times in the course of fifteen seconds, and another volunteer speaking to the room kept saying the word "Ecuas," a slur that volunteers used for Ecuadorians. At one point, she even looked at our training manager from Quito and said, "I know you guys don't like that term, but . . ."

I left the workshop feeling tired, sad, and embarrassed to be a part of the Peace Corps.

❖ ❖ ❖

ONLY A MONTH LATER I had to travel up to Quito for my training group's Mid-Service Conference. In the three weeks between the Resiliency Workshop and this event, I learned that four volunteers in my old province, Manabí, had been pulled out of their sites in response to a major drug bust that took place in the area. One volunteer, who lived in a small fishing village, was arrested because, unbeknownst to him, his landlords were major drug traffickers who'd been storing bulk amounts of cocaine on their property. Just as she did with me, Pilar immediately arrived on the scene and got the volunteer out before he could get into serious trouble. All the major newspapers around the country carried the story, pointing out that the DEA had been involved. This newest shake-up in Manabí was a hot topic during the Mid-Service Conference. It had been almost a year since Pilar and the Colonel had come to rescue me from the savagery of La Segua.

In addition to routine medical checkups, the object of the conference was to evaluate the first half of our service and make plans for our final year in site. Again, the specifics were a little shady beforehand, but one thing we could be sure of was that no group activity or team-building trope would be omitted.

The first day kicked off with a somewhat humiliating exercise: We had to stand, one by one, in front of the room and speak of the "accomplishments and/or lessons learned" from our first year in site (most people focused on their "lessons learned"). I still had a little ways to go with my grant proposal before I could turn it in for approval, so the future conditional tense was a big feature in my short speech.

On the second day we played. One of the many games involved taking a set of cards with varied descriptions of how we viewed our working relationship in our communities and lining them up in categories marked by hopscotch-like boxes taped to the floor. The session ended a full hour later with many of us still unsure of its purpose.

Another game tested our communication skills. We sat in circles of five people, and a colored sticker was put on everyone's forehead. The person with the green sticker was to be interrupted every time he or she tried to talk during the discourse. The session ended with hearty laughs all around and a reminder that we should actively listen to one another.

For a special treat, an American woman who lived in Quito—a self-proclaimed relationship expert—visited for an advice pow-wow. Her talk focused on the difficulties of communication in a cross-cultural relationship. She brought up, for instance, that in Spanish there is no real word for "rape" and the word that's used for it could also mean "annoyances" or "traffic violations."

When giving love advice, she often cited her former relationship with a Chilean man. She attributed the downfall of their courtship to the fact that every time they got in an argument, she said they needed to make a *compromiso*. She thought that she was saying "compromise," when actually she was saying a word that translates to "obligation" or "commitment"—both words that, to varying degrees, mean the opposite of what she was trying to say. (The word she was looking for—as she and all of us now knew—was *comprometer*.) I found the intersection of grammar, rhetoric, and love to be unsettling.

At the end of one day we all filled out pieces of paper that read, "Who Is Going to Keep You Accountable?" On the front of the sheet was a "Balance Wheel of Life for Peace Corps Volunteers." We had to rank several designated topics on a scale from 1 (not satisfied at all) to 10 (completely satisfied). My Balance Wheel of Life was marked thusly:

Being a Peace Corps Volunteer	2
Relationships with Counterparts	5
Family	8
Growth & Development/Spirituality	7
My Future	4
Personal Relationships/Support from Others	3
Health & Recreation	6
Other: Personal Hobbies/Creativity	9

I don't know why, but I brought this paper back to my site and it remained taped to my wall for the next forty-four weeks.

Taking the several workshops and activities into account, the theme of this conference, without a doubt, had to be *sustainability*. This was the newest buzzword in the development industry. The idea that "if you give a man a fish, he'll eat for a day but if you teach him to fish, he'll eat for life" had been around for a long time. But it seemed like it wasn't until very recently that people had been getting border-line hysterical about the fact that it wasn't development unless it was *sustainable development*. (Of course, not once does the Peace Corps or any of these other organizations address whether it is sustainable to continue teaching that man to fish for fifty years straight—with no end in sight.)

Less than a month earlier, the BP platform in the Gulf of Mexico exploded, creating one of the largest ocean oil spills in history. I sat with a friend of mine in the back of the room during another session on sustainability and discussed whose society was more sustainable: ours or Ecuador's. My friend finally said that while Ecuador's way of life was nothing to aim for, we probably came from the least sustainable society in human history.

We sat through hours and hours of more sessions about what made up sustainable methods of project development and how best to implement sustainable practices. During our lunch breaks, I checked the Internet in the volunteer lounge: At record-setting rates, crude oil continued to gush from the sea floor and spread across the water like a creepy dark cloud.

CHAPTER 38

I returned to my site after the conference and put the finishing touches on my grant proposal. It was mid-2010. I was twenty-four years old and halfway through my service. I was thinking about the future. I was analyzing the past. I was trying to get something done. I was isolated in my jungle town, the power was blacking out frequently, the Amazon pelted my area with violent thrusts of rain and heat, and once again, I spent my days cooped up indoors doing paperwork for the grant.

The single mothers living across from me spent all day cooking and doing laundry by hand and hanging it on the lines across the patio, only to have another rainstorm give it a second rinse. Out on the street, men selling coconut milk and candy belted out the destinations of the buses that passed through, even though the buses were really only headed to one of two places. My landlady's son used kerosene to burn the trash behind the property, creating flames that climbed fifteen feet into the air, licking the branches of the fruit tree above. I saw and heard and smelled all this while sitting in my apartment working away . . . on my laptop. This was just the beginning of the twenty-first-century Peace Corps experience.

In the twenty-first-century Peace Corps, your new country director spoils his political capital by pulling such stunts as cutting funding for the Gender and Development volunteer working group because things like scholarships for leadership-oriented summer camps aren't *sustainable*. And as if that weren't bad enough, volunteers are still upset about that new Whereabouts Policy and what they think is a lack of communication. It will take volunteers about a year to realize he's a good guy.

In the twenty-first-century Peace Corps, your service will see the coming and going four different country directors (two interim), two program managers, two program and training specialists, and so many others you lose count.

In the twenty-first-century Peace Corps, a yearlong investigation by the inspector general's office will cite a high rate of staff turnover in your country's post as proof of poor leadership and a reason for an inflated budget. The same report will produce evidence that the post's former country director (who left just before you arrived) sold government vehicles to local non-governmental organizations, or NGOs, for a fraction of their market value. This will eventually lead to a heavy fine and possible jail time for said former country director (who by now is working as a contractor in Afghanistan).

In the twenty-first-century Peace Corps, you learn that there is a new file format for submitting your quarterly Volunteer Report File and the directions for downloading it (let alone filling it out in Excel and submitting it to your program managers) are confusing. And where it asks for specific numbers for data such as "How many host country nationals have been trained in a capacity building skill?" or "How many people have learned at least three ways to improve their health?" you are confused by the pull-down menus even after filling out a half dozen of these things already. Mostly, you know from talking to other volunteers that they fill these forms out in a sort of highly organized bureaucratic bullshit*ese* in which it's not so important that the numbers mean anything as long as your file looks nice—that is to say, your data are aesthetically pleasing. At the end of the year, the office will design an annual report, sent out to volunteers and counterparts in both PDF and hard copy, in which the made-up numbers are compiled into graphs and statistics.

In the twenty-first-century Peace Corps, you hike off into the jungle one day with an agriculture tech from the municipality to go grafting cacao branches and she shows you how to do it, and you follow along snipping the green twigs in the same way, wandering through a forest of cacao trees hanging low like a field of giant umbrellas, and all of a sudden the agriculture tech says, "You've never done this before, have you?" and you say, "No, never; learned a little about it during our training, but—" and she says, "But you said you're a natural resources volunteer, isn't that right?" and you say, "Yes, but—" and she says, "So didn't you study this at your university?" and then you tell her that you studied government and she frowns in confusion and says, "Then why don't you work for the embassy or something?" and all you can think is *touché*, as you continue snipping away at cacao branches and eventually hike back to town.

In the twenty-first-century Peace Corps, many of the office staff in Quito come from Ecuador's educated elite class; some are more ignorant of their own country's geography and wealth disparity, and more shocked and disgusted by the living conditions at the sites, than the volunteers.

In the twenty-first-century Peace Corps everyone has to sign updated and expanded Drug and Alcohol Policies because one of the newest training groups to show up in the country really likes to party, but possibly took it too far when another volunteer reported that several of them were doing heroin while hanging out in Cuenca one weekend.

THEY APPROVED MY GRANT. THE Peace Corps and, presumably, others deep in the cogs of the Department of Agriculture determined my project was thoroughly sustainable and gave it the green light. It was mid-August.

Days later, my Banco de Guayaquil savings account, which usually never had a balance of more than the three-hundred-dollar stipend I received each month, had that, plus the seven grand for the greenhouse. It was a staggering figure to see on my account balance—more money than I was going to get from Uncle Sam when I completed my service eight months hence.

At the high school, there were handshakes and smiles and fist pumps. At the municipal offices, there were words of congratulations and a genuine sense of shock that I'd gotten all the money I said I could.

Later that week, I took the bus into Loja to see Patricio, the owner of the irrigation and greenhouse construction company that I'd contracted to do the work. I'd met with him several times over the previous four months to talk about the design and construction, including once when he said he was busy so we got in his car and talked while he dropped his wife off at work and took his kids to school on the other side of Loja.

We already had contracts with prices for materials and labor, and computer printouts with designs and layouts. I'd needed all this to write up the grant proposal, which, in its final form, had to include details like exactly how many meters of wire and how many bolts we'd use and the unit price for each. Now, at last, I had the money that I owed him to get the project started. After we sat down to finalize the agreement, I walked to the bank and wired the seven thousand dollars to his business's account. Patricio was happy. (It would end up taking the municipality of Zumbi a few months to get him the two grand that they owed him, but Patricio never seemed to mind—"I work with the government all the time," he said with a smile.)

I spent the rest of the weekend in Loja, sleeping on the futon of a volunteer who had an apartment perched up on a hill with a view of the entire city. The many times I stayed there, we ate well and had fun. I'd usually wander around the city during the day, using (slightly) faster Internet and spending money on bootlegged DVDs and getting ice cream. Then I'd get on the bus and head up over the mountain pass and back down through the cloud forest into Zumbi.

CHAPTER **39**

I t was late August. I'd been in Ecuador for seventeen months. Just over a year had passed since I was jettisoned from the coast and thrown into a shotgun marriage with this new site. And finally things were about to start happening: It was greenhouse construction day.

I felt a sense of accomplishment I didn't think I'd ever reach during my time here. Mostly, I felt vindicated for the previous year and a half of not getting anything concrete done and feeling sorry for myself about it. Now, the time had almost arrived when, in response to the people asking me what the hell I was doing in Zumbi, I could point to something and say, "That, over there, I built that."

It was, perhaps, a bit narcissistic.

I walked from my apartment up to the high school with a hop in my step. I was going to meet Carlito at the school and let him know the schedule for when the construction crew would show up and what kind of help they'd need. As I walked, I thought back to the day Carlito and the vice principal came to my apartment to suggest the project. Thank goodness I'd managed to find at least one person in this town who was interested in my help and somewhat on board with something involving the environment—someone who *got it*.

I approached the high school prepared to talk to the administrators about what a great day this was for the future of the school and the environmental awareness of the students when I saw several tractors and other machinery at work. Just past the front gate, a crew was at work chopping down a forest of trees on the school's property. Some of the trees were over forty feet tall and others you could walk up to and reach for a lemon. When I first began working with the high school, I remember thinking that this little forest on a plot of land half the size of a football field was the nicest part about their entire property. Now the trees were crashing down one by one, like colossal metaphors, and being loaded up in bundles of firewood-sized logs and shipped away.

Carlito was sitting on the front steps of the administrative building smoking cigarettes and joking around with the vice principal and a few of the school's maintenance workers. We smiled and greeted one another.

"Hey, so what's going on here?" I said, pointing to the deforesting crew a few yards to the left of us.

"Oh that. We're just making some room," said Carlito.

"For what?" I asked. We were yelling to hear over the sounds of chain saws and the splintering tree chunks.

"Actually, we need the money."

"Ah, you're selling the wood?" I said.

"Yes, and maybe we'll plant some corn there," said Carlito. He shrugged his shoulders.

Everyone paused as we watched the trees fall to the ground, creating giant swirling clouds of dust and leaves.

"Anyway," I said. "Today's a great day. The engineer from the construction company should arrive around three o'clock this afternoon to take a look at the land for the greenhouse. Will you guys be here?"

Carlito said yes.

"All right," I said. I started to say something else about getting the field ready for the greenhouse builders when Carlito interrupted me.

"Our school bus is falling apart," he said. He pointed at the bus over to our right. It was parked in the gravel in front of the main school building.

"Does it still work?" I said.

One of the workers who'd been sitting smoking chimed in. "Yes, it runs, but not very well."

"So it made me think," said Carlito, "that you could help us with another project. You could get us a new school bus. Maybe you could call some of your gringo friends at the Peace Corps or in the United States and say, 'Look, this is a good school here in Zumbi. How about you help out my friends here with the money to buy a school bus.'"

He arched his eyebrows and lifted his palms up, as if to say, *That's a reasonable proposition, don't you think?*

"But you know the Peace Corps doesn't do projects like that," I said. "The project we just did required the contributions from the school and the municipality—"

"I know, I know," he said. "I'm not talking about a gift or a handout. I'm talking about something fair, you know, where for instance we plant a few hundred trees and then you buy us a new school bus. What about that, huh?"

IT HAD BEEN EIGHT MONTHS since I'd first met Carlito while standing half naked behind my house and seven months since we'd begun the process of getting the grant written. That was a long time to spend *talking* about a greenhouse. The week before, we'd convinced the mayor to let the school use a government tractor to level out the field where we were building the thing. When the guys from Loja all showed up to build it, they spent a week in Zumbi, sleeping on cots in the classrooms at night and doing the construction during the day.

Once it was finally standing, Carlito and I, along with everyone else at the school, spent a few days just walking around inside and marveling at the thing. In the sunlight, the white plastic let off a blinding glow that you could see when you hiked into the hills around Zumbi and looked down at the town. Then the sun disappeared for days at a time and the roof repelled even the most violent of raindrops, the water neatly draining off in the roof's channels. It was a beauty.

And then the school year began.

began thinking that getting the greenhouse built was one of the biggest accomplishments of my life. I did, after all, write that whole grant, in Spanish, practically without any help. In fact, the more other people got involved, the more it usually slowed things down.

Somewhere back in that first year when I just lay around in pain and pitying myself, I'd given up on thinking that I would ever leave with something to show for my time. But now I did and so I patted myself on the back. It also gave me an incredible chip on my shoulder with respect to other volunteers. Almost all the ones I knew were doing arts and crafts with preschoolers, or giving sex education seminars that no one listened to, or—even worse—giving free labor to an already well-established NGO.

I would look at that giant hunk of metal and plastic shining in the green field behind the school and drift off to a self-aggrandizing mind orgy, fantasizing how this thing would still be standing years after I had gone. But the self-congratulatory attitude was exactly what I disliked in other volunteers, so I quickly came to my senses and realized that this was just the work I came to do, nothing more. I got over it.

Maintaining the greenhouse became a Sisyphean adventure. During the planning phases of the project, I had (admittedly) glossed over the exact details of how the outdoor science curriculum would work out. I figured we'd play it by ear. When the new school year began,

Carlito signed a contract with his teachers, who agreed to have their classes build the seed beds by a certain date, at which point he would give them the seeds and set up the irrigation access. It was that easy: The order would come down from the principal and the teachers would follow through with the students. I would be there alongside to help facilitate.

I quickly discovered that students attended school an average of only about three days a week. This wasn't just because Fridays or Mondays were taken off for a long weekend. If it wasn't a "scheduling holiday" or an entire day of "teachers' meetings" disrupting the school week, it was a teachers union parade or strike, or one of the country's several independence days, or a religious observance, or the death of a teacher's child (more "accidents" with shotguns). Three consecutive days of school were about as likely as finding a textbook in the classrooms.

Once in a while I'd get lucky and show up on a day when teachers and students were present. One teacher was enthusiastic about the greenhouse but had his own idea of how things should work. He had his students building seed beds using the rocky ground soil that could barely support the weeds sprouting from it. When I politely told him we needed to clear that out and use the nice soil the municipal government had just dropped off for us, he said, "My brother, no, no, no. We plant with this soil. Believe me, I know." The giant pile of fresh, nutrient-rich ground soil was only twenty feet from where we were standing.

Before the dirt conversation could escalate into an argument, Carlito showed up and walked inside the greenhouse, puffing on a cigarette and wiping sweat off his brow with a handkerchief. "What the hell is this?" he said. "Use that other soil! This stuff is no good. Why do you think we went through the trouble of getting this good soil delivered?"

That solved that.

Two other teachers had classes that were supposed to rotate in the greenhouse science curriculum during that first semester. One of them I never saw. I began to wonder if he'd died without anyone telling me (which actually happened a few times before, including when the owner of my apartment passed away).

The third teacher indeed existed and had spoken to me before, but quite simply refused to do the work we had agreed on. I hiked out behind the school one morning to see his class standing around outside the greenhouse. Some were aimlessly pulling weeds fifty yards away. Others were hacking away at rocks with busted shovels, looking like nineteenth-century railroad laborers. Others stood off to the side sucking on lollypops and tossing their wrappers into the creek. They all were doing anything but work in the greenhouse.

I said hello to everyone, then asked the teacher why they weren't building the seed beds and bringing in the new soil with the wheelbarrow I'd commandeered for them.

"We don't have any irrigation," said the teacher.

"Yes, we're going to set that up after the seed beds are built and we can plant the seeds and have something to water," I said.

"Oh yeah? Well, we don't have any tools either," he said.

I looked around me and saw nearly every student holding a shovel or pickax or rake that had been lent to us by families from the other classes. The fact is there were tools all over the place.

"It looks like you guys are doing all right," I said. "But I can ask Carlito to get some more tools. In the meantime, maybe we can get started inside. Your class has to build a third of these seed beds, right?"

"We don't have *any* of the things we need to get the work done," he said. He grimaced at me as if I wasn't *getting it*, which, up until that point, I wasn't. This was just a small, polite "fuck you" from an Ecuadorian teacher who was drawing a line in the sand and essentially saying, *Look, I've put up with a lot of shit in this life, but taking orders from a gringo half my age will not be one of them.*

Later on, I tried humiliation by peers—going to the other teachers and saying, Gosh, Santos's class is really falling behind schedule. But that didn't work either. The guy was a rock. When I returned one day with the vice principal, who was as incredulous as I that this teacher refused to work, I stood and watched while the teacher basically told his boss to fuck off, too.

"But Santos—Santito," the vice principal pleaded, "we all signed the agreement that your classes would do the work."

The conversation ended in a harrumph, with both men throwing their arms in the air, walking off, and basically saying screw it.

As we walked in from the field to the offices, I asked the vice principal if this sort of thing was normal. "Yeah," he said. "Some of them just don't listen."

And so my days of maintaining, training, and facilitating went just about like that. Eventually, the beds got built and the seeds got sown and the shiny new greenhouse was a pleasure to look at, as the 692 square meters bloomed into neat rows of green produce.

But somewhere along the way I did, in fact, begin to feel an enormous sense of guilt. I started feeling like this was one big handout. What would these people actually learn from it? Only the strategy of waiting with their hands out the next time a gringo or an NGO came through town. I thought more about sustainability, of course. In my most pessimistic moments, I decided that nothing was sustainable anymore. If the money or ideas came from an outside invasion, how sustainable could it really be?

I began thinking that it was my own ego or greed or that I just wanted so badly to get a real project in the ground to call my own and feel like I had made a mark of some kind. At the same time, I'd seen plenty of community health or sustainable agriculture volunteers who ended up just drinking with their neighbors for two years. So while I was driven in part by selfishness, I guess I was also driven to not be like them.

In a way, I could justify the fact that I wasn't in there every day working hands-on with the classes. After all, one day I would leave and they'd have to do it all on their own anyway. This tapering down of direct involvement in projects was one of the methods of sustainable development that we'd been trained about.

But it tore me up thinking about how I'd gloated to myself that I built this structure—this monument to condescending foreign aid—and then didn't have the emotional energy to follow through and tangle with the teachers and everyone else on a daily basis about what should go on inside the thing.

CHAPTER 41

If there was anything in the world of international development sexier than the idea of *sustainability*, it was *ecotourism*. Not just tourism—which was almost like a bad word compared with its new-age cousin—but *eco*tourism. I, of course, had an up-close run-in with this phenomenon with Juan and company during my dark, brief adventure in La Segua. That was far from the last I would hear of it. Not only was ecotourism a term bound to come up several dozen times in any conversation about Ecuador (about half the Ecuadorian college graduates I ever came across had degrees in ecotourism, like Juan), but it seemed that the majority of volunteers were working on an ecotourism project in one form or another.

In the final year of my service, I saw a television documentary produced by one of Quito's news stations. It told the story of a town of only a few hundred in the northern Amazon region where the suicide rate among locals was several times greater than the world average. People were killing themselves left and right. The town was responsible for producing lots of naranjilla, a sweet fruit grown in that area of the Amazon. The report went on to explain how the locals used an especially toxic pesticide to grow the naranjilla and how because they either couldn't read the directions or were being illegally sold too much of the pesticide, they were essentially poisoning themselves when they worked with—and later consumed—the fruit. The report went on to suggest that the overdose of chemicals from the pesticide was playing a role in the alarmingly high rates of depression and suicide.

The people in that town just needed someone to provide a safer option for growing the naranjilla, and it could literally start saving lives. We did happen to have a Peace Corps volunteer there for quite some time, but she was working in ecotourism.

And so after a year and a half in Ecuador, I'd sat through too many ecotourism seminars to count. I began to think it was mostly a cruel trick being played on the people there—leading them to believe Ecuador could be the next Costa Rica. Leading them to believe that ecotourism was their golden ticket to prosperity. Leading the poor farmers who lived in three-quarters deforested towns like mine to believe they could build a path to a waterfall and the gringos and their dollars would start raining in.

Ironically, it was only a month after I'd attended another disappointing ecotourism conference at the municipal building when my area of the province actually did attract some visitors—though not in a good way.

About ten minutes east of Zumbi, on the only road leading from the town out of the province to the south, the most unusual bridge spans the Yacuambi River. Made of concrete, it has just one lane, causing traffic buildup on both ends, as cars and buses wait for others to cross ahead of them one at a time. But that isn't the strangest part. The bridge is concave in shape, meaning it slopes downward with its lowest point midway over the river. The rollercoaster effect created by speeding down one side and coasting up the other makes for an exhilarating few seconds, but has also resulted in several accidents. Every person or product that goes to the town from elsewhere in the province must cross this bridge.

The whole time I'd been in Zumbi, workers had been constructing a new bridge about a hundred yards upstream from the concave one. As much as the ancient single-lane concrete bridge was underdoing it, this new bridge, you could say, was overdoing it. It was a monster, an Amazonian Golden Gate, spanning a river that was no more than ten feet deep and thirty yards wide.

Considering how splendid this structure was, President Correa was scheduled to come down for the ribbon-cutting ceremony when it was completed.

But he never came.

Three days before his visit, the new bridge collapsed, spraying giant scraps of metal and rebar and blocks of concrete into the river and killing one of the construction workers in the fall. For months, while a new team of engineers tried to fix it, the grotesque and twisted heap looked like a Transformer that had lain down to die in the flowing brown river.

After the collapse, every time buses crossed the tiny concrete concave bridge—now considered by far to be our safest river-crossing option—people would hang out the window snapping pictures or simply gawking at the pathetic wreckage. We finally had our tourist attraction.

It was things like this that I spent my final months in Ecuador being cynical about, while working here and there with the teachers in the greenhouse and continuing my love-hate relationship with Ecuador and my battle against immense boredom in Zumbi. Somewhere in there, I read *Atlas Shrugged* in just a few days.

CHAPTER 42

And so you're here all alone doing close to nothing and the time passes. You're not even sure how, but it does. And the days feel like they'll never end, but the weeks become a blur.

And here you are, measuring your life not in coffee spoons, but in dishes washed, good conversations had, baskets of laundry done by hand, walks down the dusty road to swim in the river, cold showers that are *good* cold showers because it's hot as hell and from the bathroom you can look through the crack between the brick and the corrugated tin and see the green foothills surrounding the small valley.

You measure it in rolls of bread bought for five cents apiece at the bakery down the road. You measure it in ice cream bars bought on hot days for a quarter. You measure it in Saturdays spent drinking bad beer—except it's good beer because it's light and cold and you can drink it in the shade and watch the grainy TV in the corner while the women behind the counter ask you questions about the world. You measure it in plates of rice and chicken—which still have way too much rice and not enough chicken—and all you can think after eating it so many times is how it's not so much food as just something you joylessly insert into your stomach to survive.

You measure it in books read, which eventually comes out to 152 overall, or 1.46 per week. You measure it in Friday nights spent alone because going out to drink with any men in town is an exercise in patience that you don't have. You measure it in Saturday nights spent sitting on the bench in front of your building and staring at the people and cars going by and wondering where you belong. You measure it in festivals, which seem to be every month because there are celebrations for not just the country or the province or the town, but also for the high schools and the preschools and the neighborhoods. You go to these and you drink and dance and then spend the next six months hearing your neighbors give recaps of every girl you danced with and which ones you are sure to impregnate and consequently marry and stay with forever. And when it briefly crosses your mind that staying here forever wouldn't be a bad idea, you pause for a moment and become disgusted with yourself.

You see a woman in town who is absolutely gorgeous—*super-model* gorgeous. But then you find out she is sixteen years old. And if that's not enough to stop you, you find out she is married. And if *that's* not enough to stop you, you find out she has a child. Although the others are not quite as gorgeous, this is a similar scenario that happens over and over. More grown-up-looking beauties make eyes at you and then you see them in the classroom at the high school. Or you see them walking down the street another time and now they're nursing a baby. It all makes you start to wonder that if you were going to find one of these beauties to settle down with, what window of opportunity—if any—was there? They're beautiful and underage, but by the time they turn eighteen and become available, it seems they've already popped out a baby or two. And, by the way, the rapid aging continues—you'll come across thirty-year-olds who look fifty and sixty-year-olds who look eighty-five. (Then you confirm that this phenomenon is not due to any bias or racism on your part, because when neighbors are shown pictures of *your* parents, who are in their late fifties, the neighbors believe them to be no older than forty.) It must be, as they say, something in the water.

There are good nights visiting other volunteers and cooking Mexican food and exchanging three-month-old copies of *The New Yorker*. There are bad nights wondering how many times you're going to eat stale tuna or pasta for dinner. There are good mornings, when the sun is shining in through the slats on the ceiling and you can feel the warmth heating up the bedroom and you can feel the light wind pushing back through the torn curtains on the far side of the room. Then there are bad mornings when the rainwater is already flooding in through the bedroom door and you must unclog leaves and broken glass and old shoes from the drain outside before you can even wade to the bathroom. There are days you put on sunscreen and you're proud of yourself for remembering and then there are days you walk down to the river without it and that stinging redness when you get back probably erases all the times you lathered up with high SPF.

There is a calendar on the wall and turning the page over to a new month is nothing if not a satisfying and glorious feeling. But then you feel bad about counting down the months or weeks or days because you realize that this is life. It doesn't get much realer than this, and counting the days is like marching toward death.

There are more festivals and there are also holidays, including lots of Catholic ones, which, judging by the grim atmosphere and low-hanging heads and slumped shoulders on the people shuffling into the chapel, aren't necessarily what you'd consider holidays.

There are hikes into the jungle at almost every opportunity because your friends in town nearly all have a parcel of land out there and the parts that aren't deforested for grazing are exquisite. There are clear creeks and tall trees and giant green leaves and gullies and caves with bats and rock walls and birds and monkeys in the distance. And there are waterfalls where you can take your clothes off and jump into water so cold that it takes your breath away.

There are walks around town in the morning, with you saying hello to the neighbors or going to shoot your basketball alone behind the elementary school. There are walks around town in the afternoons, with you spitting sunflower seeds and stopping in to talk with the old ladies and single mothers who make up your friends. And there are walks around town at night, with just the stars overhead and the teenagers flirting and making out while sitting on curbs in dark alleyways, because they sure as hell can't get away with that at home. You spend hours and hours of every day . . . walking. No one has simply *walked* the length and breadth of Zumbi and its surrounding *barrios* as many times as you have. On the walks, your mind spins through time, like a hand reaching into a shoebox to pull out the faded Polaroid memories.

There are letters home. In the beginning there were more and now you hardly have the energy to go through the motions of *explaining* everything. But you write some anyway.

There are rides in the back of pickup trucks with all the jungle around you. You look at the water rushing by and the lush plants shooting up out of the red dirt and you pass by old men on the road walking back to town in their rubber boots and overalls. You hit the potholes, stop for the cattle, and hear the *cumbia* music blaring from the car speakers and you think, *Now, NOW, I'm in Latin America.*

And these are the moments of transcendence. These are the moments when you feel the levity in your chest—when you see all the people passing by and you can't help thinking that they are human and surely trying to just live their lives with some sort of dignity and that that's the only thing that really matters. Sure, soon enough you will go back to cursing them for being too slow or ignorant or rude or overly curious about you. But then you will have another transcendent moment in the back of a pickup truck or in the window seat of another bus ride or on another walk along the river, and you'll feel tremendous guilt about the bitterness and the anger and frustration.

And so life pushes on, even in Zumbi.

There's a girl who lives on your street, whom you see every day at school working in the greenhouse. She has everyone talking about her because she's gotten caught letting old men fondle her out by the soccer fields for fifty dollars.

You're on a bus ride from Loja to Zumbi—a ride you will end up taking eighty-five times total during your time here—and you're sitting next to an indigenous woman with a child on her lap. The child is wearing tattered clothes and his cheeks are sunburned and his eyes are crusty and he's getting carsick. (And you can't blame him because the driver is swerving down the mountain like a fucking lunatic.) So the mother holds the tip of her long black ponytail up to his nose saying, "Sniff it, sniff it. There, come on, sniff it!" And she repeats it over and over, shoving it under the little boy's runny nose. Finally, he sniffs it.

Here you are, going about life as usual, and still occasionally feeling that brief but crippling pain in the balls and from deep within your man plumbing.

Then it's another year and you have another birthday and are officially into the realm of when birthdays are neither here nor there. It's just time marching on.

Here you are at a going-away party for the beautiful doctor who originally dealt with your balls and gave you the injection at the community health center. Some of the men there are talking about how pretty she is and one of them turns to you and says, among a series of winks and nods, "Yeah, Grigsby, you should tell *la doctora* that you have the same problem"—he points to your balls—"and that you need her to 'check you out' again." Everyone at the party, including you, erupts into laughter, because in this life, you can choose to either laugh or cry.

And speaking of your balls: From time to time you're in the next town over and you keep seeing the lab technician with the swastika tattoo on her wrist and you briefly wonder if she truly exists or if she is only in your imagination.

There are more floods and suicides and landslides and car wrecks. One weekend, Zumbi's mayor nearly dies when he "falls asleep" behind the wheel at 4 a.m., crashing through a guardrail and rolling his car into a ditch.

Then your next-door neighbor has a baby. The baby is cute and you like to hold him in your arms and talk to him in English, which makes all the single mothers living nearby hoot and holler with laughter.

And then, like most days, there's the other neighbor boy, Steven, rushing into your apartment to ask you about any and all things gringo. Today he wants to know the meaning of the English term "mission accomplished."

Here you are finally taking morning jogs again, because with diet changes, warm-water soakings and a switch to briefs, the testicular pain has abated. As you're running up the hills, dodging cattle and stray dogs, you wonder if you dropped dead out there, how long it would be before anyone realized it.

Here you are walking between your apartment and the high school every day to check on the greenhouse. And on the walk, you always pass by a different, older greenhouse that was built with the help of another Peace Corps volunteer a decade earlier. The years have not been kind to this greenhouse: With its metal frame exposed and its sad tattered plastic flapping about in the breeze, it looks like the rotting carcass of one of those elephants that goes off to die alone on the Serengeti. The people who run this particular greenhouse approached you about giving—yes, *giving*—them the money to repair it, and one time this lady happened to approach you on a bad day and the conversation deteriorated into you saying that it was perhaps time for them to think of ways to raise money that didn't include asking foreigners to give it to them. "Are you going to just keep asking for money?" you said. She looked back at you with a confused gaze, but it turns out it was a productive conversation after all, because they ended up raising the money themselves. But in the meantime, you continually pass by the dying greenhouse carcass and all you can think is how you're staring into a former volunteer's project and also into the future of yours. So you think: This is what foreign aid looks like.

On September 30, 2010, there is a coup attempt in Quito. The national police force attempts to throw President Rafael Correa out of office. Even though their salaries have increased fivefold during his administration, the police are upset about a bill that would make it harder for them to achieve seniority and get raises. (Correa's response: They clearly hadn't read the bill.)

There are tires burning in the streets. There is tear gas thrown. There are half-assed attempts at looting in metropolitan streets. For several hours, Correa is barricaded inside a Quito hospital, protected by the military. At one point during the day, he shouts down from a hospital window that if they want to kill the president they should come and get him (which was pretty cool). Later that night, after Correa makes a heroic escape from the hospital and at least one police officer is blown away on live television, he gives a rousing speech to his supporters from the balcony of the presidential palace, where speakers and giant television screens are already set up when he arrives. During the whole day, life in Zumbi goes on as normal and people watch this all go down on the restaurants' TV sets as if it were a soccer match.

You briefly date a woman who grew up an hour from Zumbi but studies modern art at a university in Loja. The two of you spend some days hanging out and eating lunch and swimming in the river together. But after a while, you lose touch. And one day, months later after you've drifted apart, you're on the bus to Loja and she gets on and sits down next to you. You spend the next two hours talking. And at one point she's telling you about her studies and her life and her goals and she's smiling and she's beautiful and she says something that hits you and doesn't go away: "I don't want to live like my parents live." So then you see her a few weeks later and you spend the day making out and walking through a park in Loja.

You experience your second and final New Year's Eve in Ecuador. You go with a group of friends for a trip to the beach. You get drunk and eat good food and laugh and play cards and lie in the sand and get sunburned. And upon returning to Zumbi, you find that a neighbor has reported you to the police because he is worried that you're going to poison his dog to death. (It's because late one night, when his dog was barking so violently that you thought something dreadful was taking place, you went over to ask him if he could please quiet the dog.) The complaint is filed at the police station—where the neighbor's sister is the clerk—and you have to go in and explain that in addition to not being a dog murderer, you're actually an animal lover (which is a phrase that may or may not translate well into Spanish).

CHAPTER 43

More months melted together and I got tired.

I was tired of the kid next door lighting things on fire right outside my bedroom window. When the little arsonist wasn't playing with matches, he was getting violent with the other neighbor's kitten or baby boy.

I was tired of the mother across the patio screaming at her kids day and night. Her eighteen-year-old niece, who lived next door to them, smacked around her four-year-old in gusts of anger that echoed throughout the patio and startled me from dozens of yards away.

I was just tired. No matter what I tried, I couldn't peel myself out of bed until I'd gotten a solid nine hours of sleep, often slumbering right on through the neighbor's blaring techno music that lasted from six to seven every morning.

I was tired of people who'd known me for nearly two years staring at me and asking where I was from and if I spoke English.

I was tired of baking banana bread at the kitchen down the road and having the woman there tell me I was doing it wrong. I've made this about a hundred times and I'm reading right from the recipe, I'd say. She'd shake her head like I was an idiot and then ask, "What's this food called?"

I was tired of people asking me if Alaska was its own country and when I said it was actually part of the U.S., having them laugh at me and call me stupid.

I was tired of people asking me for the thirtieth time what I did there. "You know the new greenhouse your child works in every day at school? I got that built." They stared back at me in dumb amusement with the hollow eyes of poverty.

I was tired of people asking me why I didn't have a girlfriend there. I wanted to say it's because I prefer girls with full sets of teeth or fewer than three children. But I never said any of it. I let them call me a faggot and continued on with my day.

I was tired of the heat blisters that developed on my ass cheeks. I rubbed on cortisone every night to stop the itching and doused my underwear with baby powder in the mornings. But the itchiness never went away.

I was tired of people asking me when I was leaving and then asking why I didn't stay and live there forever. Have you taken a look around? I wanted to say. You've managed to turn a piece of the Amazon into a bald, sweltering cloud of leaded diesel fumes.

I was tired of the landlady's son, a slightly mentally handicapped alcoholic in his late thirties, asking me if I wanted to go to the whorehouse with him. He spent every evening getting drunk in the park then wandering around town trying to coax others into drinking whisky with him. Like a lot of things, the image of him going to the whorehouse and dropping seven dollars for twenty minutes with an underage girl was sad and surreal.

I was tired of finding cockroaches in my cereal and in my shoe and on my dresser and in my bed.

I was tired of being tired.

I was tired of explaining that colds and the flu are caused by viruses, not changes in the weather or from drinking cold drinks on hot days.

I was tired of my body. After several months of thinking that I had just a bad case of swamp ass, the Peace Corps doctor discovered that it was, in fact, a simple fungal infection requiring the same cream used for athlete's foot. It turns out that standing in front of a fan in the nude every time I got out of the shower that whole time was doing me no good.

And my armpits smelled like the meat section in an open-air market.

And I had amoebas again and this time didn't even realize it for a few months.

I was tired of taking notes of all the things that were making me tired; I worried it was making me callous.

I was tired of waking up in the mornings and feeling like crying from the loneliness.

I was tired of people being nice to me and asking me questions about my family and where I was from because I knew that soon I would leave and never come back.

I was tired of the threatening letters from the Peace Corps doctors to all of us reminding that if we didn't take our malaria medication, we'd be Medically Separated. I taped the letters on my wall, next to the four unopened medicine bottles of doxycyclene sitting on my windowsill.

I was tired of the policeman taking his gun out of its holster and aiming it at my face "for fun" every time he saw me.

I was tired of the whole town mourning a teenage boy who got killed by a truck. That's what happens when fourteen-year-olds drive motorcycles on the highway, I wanted to say.

I was tired of feeling cruel.

I was tired of heartbroken teenagers getting drunk and jumping off the bridge because their girlfriends had left them.

I was tired of workers on the roof of the building next to mine getting electrocuted to death.

I was tired of people who were unemployed and spoke no English and had never traveled outside their own country telling me that my country was racist for denying them a travel visa.

I was tired of walking up to the high school and seeing new holes torn in the greenhouse's plastic and mesh netting (apparently the ju-venile lust for vandalism is universal). It made me think more and more that they didn't deserve to have the greenhouse. I fantasized about tearing the place to pieces right before I left town for good and leaving them with nothing but a pile of trash where the structure once stood. But it turned out I didn't have the energy to follow through on that either.

I was tired of some people in Zumbi thinking they were better than other people there just because they made fifty dollars more a month, or because their skin was one shade lighter, or because their cinder-block house had two bedrooms instead of one, or because their family came from the sierra.

I was tired of seeing babies get dropped.

I was tired of seeing people who were indeed poor because they were too lazy to get a job or an education when the opportunities were available.

Then I was tired of seeing people who *did* work hard but didn't realize that they were poor, in part, because their poverty contributed to others' wealth and because governments like it this way and because it's a system where there will always be a ceiling on some people's prosperity.

I was tired of being asked if, in addition to English and Spanish, I spoke "Colombian."

I was tired of the way things seemed to drone on without an end.

Yes, I was tired. And all the while, I had no idea that one day I would be back home in the U.S. but it wouldn't feel like home, and I'd feel so empty and confused that I would wish I had never left.

CHAPTER 44

For my first Thanksgiving in Ecuador, the year before, I traveled north to another Peace Corps site in the jungle where a group of volunteers met for a giant feast. While there, we met up with some Shuar Indians and I pointed out that—just like the Pilgrims—we were having our first Thanksgiving with real Native Americans. People rolled their eyes. The bus ride home—the distance from Philadelphia to Washington, D.C.—took me seventeen hours.

· The following year, I had an uneventful Thanksgiving with about ten other volunteers in Loja. We drank lots of tequila and went to bed early.

The next day in the bus station, I bought my ticket back to Zumbi and waited near the turnstile. Ten feet away, a tall man began staring at me. He didn't take his eyes off me, even when I occasionally glanced back and caught him staring. He was partially bald, which was unusual in Ecuador. He seemed to be smirking at me as though he knew something I didn't know. At his side he held a small handbag. And no matter where I looked or who else passed by or what else happened, he kept staring.

I turned around, walked twenty steps, and paid five cents to go to the terminal's bathroom. I used the urinal, washed my hands, and walked out. The man was still staring at me, eerily smiling like he wanted to put a knife into my gut. He'd repositioned himself in the terminal. Now he was over by a snack stand, still never taking his eyes off me.

I walked outside to the front of the terminal where taxis drop people off. I acted like I was waiting for someone to pick me up or for someone to arrive and meet me. I stood with my back to the brick wall so I could see anyone walking in or out of the terminal. A minute later the man came outside, glanced at me like he would enjoy hurting me, and stood out by the curb still clutching the handbag at his side. He didn't stare at me while we were outdoors, but he stood and looked back at me every now and then, waiting to see what I did next.

When he wasn't looking, I slipped back inside the terminal, went through the turnstile, and boarded my bus. It was parked at the platform and was leaving in ten minutes.

I sat down in my seat and waited. Looking out my window, past the turnstile, and into the terminal, I could see the man standing in the same place I'd first seen him. Now he was looking around and peering out toward the bus platforms like he was searching for me. I wanted the bus to leave faster. I wanted it to leave *now* before the man spotted me again. I clenched my fists and dug my heels into the floor hoping that the fucking bus would get moving.

A minute later, the bus engine rumbled on and we pulled out of the station. I exhaled and pulled my iPod from my backpack and put in the earphones. The bus got closer to the exit. On the way to the gate to leave the station, it stopped. Two girls had run after it and flagged us down. They looked relieved that the bus hadn't left without them as they climbed on to find their seats. Just behind them, also getting on the bus and passing through the door to find a seat, was the man who'd been staring at me. He still had his handbag. It was small but looked heavy. His purple T-shirt was stained with sweat.

The two girls quickly found seats. The Staring Man slowly walked toward the back of the bus, bracing himself on each of the seatbacks as he stepped forward. Now I was staring at *him*. When he passed by the row I was seated in, he paused and looked me in the eye and smirked as if to say, *I found you, motherfucker.* I win. His face was red and shiny, dotted with beads of sweat. His eyes seemed to burn and grow darker when he looked directly at me. The grin lingered on his face as he walked on past to an empty seat toward the back.

I decided not to fall asleep on this bus ride. The man sat down directly behind me, six rows back. I could see his reflection ahead of me in the window that led to the driver's cab. One hour became two, and the man still had not taken his eyes off the back of my head. I would slump down in my seat so I could still see his tall frame poking up above the other passengers but he couldn't see me.

I hid money in my shoes. I hid my ID and ATM cards deep in my backpack on the floor between my legs. I wrung my hands together. If this man got off the bus with me in Zumbi, I was going to take a running swing at him and break his nose, then sprint to find one of the policemen I knew. I was going to punch the man so hard his legs would go limp and he'd be lying there on the sidewalk when the police came to get him.

After two hours the bus was pulling into the Zamora terminal for a brief stop before continuing on to Zumbi. The man was still staring at me and smirking and clutching the small handbag in his arms.

I jumped up, grabbed my backpack, and stepped down off the bus. I walked quickly to the far end of the platform and paid five cents again to go into the bathroom. I had to go for the entire ride but didn't use the bus's urinal because I would have had to walk to the back of the bus, which meant passing the Staring Man on the way.

I heard the honk of my bus as it pulled out of the lot. I left the bathroom and jogged through the parking lot to catch it. I kept my head down as I found my seat, but I peeked toward the back and was pretty sure the man wasn't there anymore. I sat down and put my backpack on the floor. I looked around the bus. I looked out the window. I looked at the reflection in the front window. The man wasn't seated behind me.

We headed out of the station and down the avenue toward the bridge that led out of town. Three blocks away, as we neared the bridge, I looked out the window and saw the Staring Man. He stood there on the street like he was waiting and watching for something. My bus passed. I looked at him. He saw me and cocked his head sideways as he stared back. He smiled at me this time—a really sick, dark smile—and kept his eyes on me until my bus crossed the bridge and turned out of view.

An hour later, my bus dropped me off in Zumbi. I went inside my apartment and locked the door.

CHAPTER 45

I n 2011, I turned twenty-five. And the United States Peace Corps turned fifty. As I entered the final four months of my service, headquarters began bombarding us with magazine articles, videos, emails, and photos to remind us. It was exactly a half century earlier that President Kennedy announced he would send Americans to the poorest parts of the world to alleviate poverty and create intercultural understanding. (These parts of the world, the third world, also happened to be vital grounds for the Cold War raging between us, the first world, and the Communist Soviets in the second world, but that's another story.) Coincidentally, Sargent Shriver, President Kennedy's brother-in-law and the Peace Corps' first director, passed away in January.

This year also marked the agency's forty-ninth in Ecuador. It and one or two other countries had been along for pretty much the whole ride. And they had no exit strategy. Lots of people—usually either former volunteers who were overcome with nostalgia or current volunteers who hadn't thought about it very critically—considered this a reason to rejoice. Many of them, including dozens of associations of former volunteers back home, were still calling for Congress to *double* Peace Corps.

I was starting to believe that, like most humans turning fifty, the Peace Corps should begin thinking about retirement. Good god—five decades of young white people coming to this country to teach poor people to improve their lives.

Eventually, people have just got to figure it out on their own. Eventually, they *want* to figure it out on their own—and I saw this everywhere. It sounded like this: "Thank you for the money, gringo, now please fuck off."

There's a time to help and when you do it, it's virtuous. But what is perhaps more virtuous is having the wisdom to know when it's time to step back and let humans do it themselves, their way, after all the years of training. A half century of gringos giving health seminars and planting trees and teaching to recycle—how much longer must it go on, I wondered. Apparently forever. When I first arrived in Ecuador, about 130 volunteers were there; midway through my service, that number ballooned up to around 200.

WITH THREE MONTHS LEFT, I joined other volunteers from my training group and traveled to Quito for one final conference. Of the forty-four of us who arrived in the country, only twenty-eight remained, with about a half dozen of those planning to extend their service in one way or another.

The Peace Corps put us up in an Italian villa–style hotel that sat on a sprawling piece of property looking over a valley in the wealthy outskirts of Quito. The place had a pool, where on our first night we had a fancy dinner banquet with the office staff, followed by a "special surprise" that turned out to be a mariachi band (yes, the Mexican kind) kicking off an impromptu dance party. I stood off to the side after overeating.

Part of the purpose of this conference was to prepare us for life after service. One session included some staff members delivering a chilling seminar about the terrors of returning to the States. We learned that it would be harder than ever to find a job and people would ask us questions about our service and not really care to hear the answers. Then we'd get sick of talking about it anyway. The effects of reverse culture shock were real and more terrifying than anything we could imagine, so we needed to avoid grocery stores at all costs if we wanted to avert a public meltdown at the overwhelming number of *choices*.

The U.S. government would pay for three therapy sessions to deal with any "readjustment issues." The mix of emotions from leaving here and entering the U.S. at this stage of our lives could and would be crippling. And—oh yeah—before they could actually let us out of the country, we'd have to deal with more paperwork than we ever thought possible. In fact, there was a hulking document stapled together for us, which turned out to be . . . just the checklist for all the *other* paperwork we had to complete.

There were a bunch of chitchats and focus sessions that week about where the Peace Corps was and where it should go—as if it mattered and as if someone higher up would say, "Oh yes, I hadn't thought of it that way, but you're right, we should completely refocus the way we've conducted business for the last half century." Everyone had always had an opinion on the Peace Corps. But now it was as though completing two years of service had given us a certain authority or power that morphed opinion into fact—as though we had earned a PhD in all things Peace Corps, allowing us to profess on the way *things should be.*

Some—actually most—thought we should downsize and somehow attract more "highly skilled" volunteers (no one acknowledged the fact that under this requisite, nearly everyone present would have been denied during the application process). Some thought we should forget the ambassadorial stuff and dedicate the program strictly to concrete and sustainable development goals (perhaps forgetting that this already exists and it's called USAID and it is perpetually disorganized and underfunded). Others thought we should forget the "work" component—you can imagine how *their* two years went—and focus on volunteers having good times in faraway communities while facilitating cultural exchange and understanding.

Some wanted more of the Peace Corps in every way. A few liked the organization just the way it was but didn't really expound much beyond that. Almost none, however, thought that as it was currently structured and organized, the Peace Corps should continue in Ecuador.

Some, when I caught them alone and in moments of honesty, agreed that half a century is an awfully long time to be showing people how it's done. The invariable rebuttal to this is that "there are a few really great projects here and there." Yes, there will always be those few good projects. But we're talking about five decades, or two generations—or more—of Ecuadorians being treated to the worldly generosity of the white man. When does it stop?

One morning, the country director informed us that at the end of the year, Peace Corps Ecuador would discontinue its sustainable agriculture program. Although the program had been a staple of the Ecuador post for most, if not all, of its forty-nine years there (and probably the least wishy-washy in its goals), many countries worldwide were under orders to cut one of their programs. He said that lots of the agricultural themes would be folded into the community health program ("food security" was the buzzword now in contemporary international development speak).

The director also talked about their plans in the coming months to implement an English-teaching program, for which they'd secured the funding long before learning that agriculture would be cut. So much for the *real* development work I'd always associated with the Peace Corps.

In any event, as of December, the agricultural program in Ecuador would be no more. Alas, we were in the waning days of gringos telling poor people how to farm, only to have them smile, turn around, and continue with the way they'd been doing it for hundreds of years.

As with the many injustices before it, my group of departing volunteers absorbed this *coup de main* as a personal insult, which it kind of was, since the decision to eliminate agriculture was based at least in part on program results. As the director spoke, they were speechless. Later in the day during coffee breaks, each launched into bouts of nostalgia, as if the agricultural program were a dying human, followed by sentimental self-praise at all the remarkable things the program had done over the years.

The next day, I had my final medical checkup in the office. I gave another fecal sample; I got another physical; the doctor listened to my heart, thought I might have a heart murmur, then said never mind; I carried a urine sample of mine across town in a bag and it broke open and got all over me and I just laughed (two years earlier I would have cursed); I took a blood test (all clear!); I got some good food in my stomach but wondered what the point was since in a couple of months I'd be back in the U.S. gorging burritos at an alarming rate.

After another day in the big city, we all returned for our final weeks in site.

CHAPTER 46

At the beginning of my last week in Zumbi, Carlito asked me to stop by the high school that Thursday for a little ceremony they were hosting. The little ceremony turned out to include every student, teacher, and faculty member, in addition to the mayor, all the city council members, and a number of others from the municipality.

They presented me with a large engraved plaque thanking me for all the work I'd done to improve the conditions at their glorious educational institution. The thing was enormous; I could barely hold it in one hand.

After the principal made his introductory comments, thanked me, and presented me with the plaque, it was my turn to speak. The mayor, councilmen, and I were sitting up on a stage facing the rest of the students and faculty, who were sitting on plastic chairs—melting under the sun and squinting from the glare reflecting off the concrete basketball court.

I stepped up to the podium and looked out at them. I saw kids yawning and the makeup dripping off older women's faces. Some held parasols and pieces of paper over their heads to block the sun. I felt weak in the knees thinking about what I'd say next—in Spanish—to these hundreds of people who came out here. But also, it was times like these that I felt guilty about all the bitterness and resentment I'd harbored and bitched about over the years. I glanced at the politicians and back out at the people.

"First, let me thank you all for this ceremony today. Thank you for coming. But more importantly, let me thank you for the opportunity to live with you, work with you, and be a part of your community these last couple of years. It's been a pleasure.

"Right now, I'd like to say something briefly to the students who are here." I turned to where some of the uniformed kids were playing an impromptu game of soccer and some of them paused and looked up at the podium. "I've had the experience of a lifetime here: The opportunity to travel to a country far from my own, with different people and a different language, and where I knew nobody. It's changed my life. And the key to being able to do it was education. I'm telling you right now that education is the most important thing in your life. And you need to value it. There are many people here who value education." I turned toward the politicians, including the mayor, who'd gone to this high school. I nodded to the principal. Then I looked back at the students. "So if you want to have an opportunity like I've had, or if you want to open doors in your life, the answer is education. From here, I hope you all go on to the university and focus on something that will allow you to come back afterward and improve your lives, your families' lives, and your community. Thank you all again and thank you, Zumbi."

I had no idea where that came from.

God knows what I would've come up with if I'd known I was going to give a speech or had any time to prepare. But that's what I needed to say. I walked to the other side of the stage and sat down and listened as the mayor proceeded to take the microphone and speak for forty-five minutes about how his administration was dedicated to improving the school, mainly in the form of a large metal covering to go over the basketball court where the audience was currently wilting away in the Amazonian sun.

✧ ✧ ✧

MY FINAL WEEKS IN ZUMBI were the same as the rest—but just a little bit hotter and a little bit slower. Although I was ready to leave Ecuador, and had indeed been counting down the days for quite a while, I was scared shitless about returning to the U.S.

Sure, things would be nicer and more comfortable and more efficient, but I'd also had conversations with people like my dad, who said such things as, "Grigs, I'm telling ya, I've got the greenest lawn in the entire cul-de-sac; it is, literally, the envy of *everyone*," and I knew this would present its own problems.

While I walked around town spitting sunflower seeds and talking to people, everything from the previous years came rushing at me in waves. It came in mixtures of nostalgia and disbelief and good old *holy shit, I can't believe it.* But every time I tried to think of something profound—a way to sum it up in an introspective climax—the more it just seemed like a lot of lonely nights cooking bad pasta for dinner, soaking my balls in tepid water, and listening to Bob Dylan albums.

On my last weekend in Zumbi—before I rode up out of the jungle to Loja for the final time and flew from Loja to Quito to take care of Peace Corps paperwork and then flew out of Quito once and for all—there was a drive-by shooting in Zumbi, just on the other side of the bridge leading into town. Two men were murdered and their girlfriends, both holding babies, were injured by bullet fragments. The shots were fired in the middle of the night. But I didn't find out about it until the next day, because I'd been busy in my apartment having safe sex with an aerobics instructor from Loja with a seahorse tattoo on her upper back.

ACKNOWLEDGMENTS

Many people helped make this book happen, but I would like to begin by singling out two who were instrumental in my becoming a writer in the first place. Thank you to G. Brown for being a friend, mentor, and editor all these years, and to Pam Bond-Simmons, the best teacher anyone could possibly ask for.

Numerous others gave their time, endured rough drafts, and lent advice when this was a manuscript—or just an idea. My deepest gratitude goes to my brother, Andrew Crawford. Many thanks to Brenna Mannion and Clare Fieseler, as well as to Robert Bombard, Spencer Beighley, and Leslie Dressler.

And much appreciation to the rest of my family: Kent, Rick, Alison, Claire, Zuma, and Watson.

Before this was even a book, it was a difficult and lonely adventure. I owe another round of thanks to all those mentioned for their love and encouragement during that time.

A few passages from this book originated as emails sent home. Thank you to everyone who tolerated them in their inboxes.

I owe many thanks to my editor, Sandra Jonas, for her professionalism, wisdom, and expertise throughout the editing process and for catching all my errors.

More thank-yous for support go to Ryan Mazin, Amy Herdy, Jessica Case, Justin Schoolmaster, Jason Meininger, and Matt Devlin.

ABOUT THE AUTHOR

J. GRIGSBY CRAWFORD grew up in the American West and graduated with honors from George Washington University. His writing has been published in numerous newspapers, magazines, and blogs, covering everything from politics and sports to men's fashion and the environment. In April 2011 Crawford completed his Peace Corps service and returned to the United States. Since that time, his man plumbing has been mostly pain-free. He now lives peacefully in Washington, D.C. *The Gringo* is his first book. Visit his website at www.jgrigsby.com.

CPSIA information can be obtained at www.ICGtesting.com
Printed in the USA
LVOW101036100513

333161LV00002B/42/P